D1554954

Breathe New Life Into Your Job and Get
Equipped, Empowered **and** Engaged!

THE INSPIRED CAREER

By
Jeffrey D. Hatchell, MBA

The best is yet to come!

Jeffrey D. Hatchell

emerge
publishing

TULSA, OKLAHOMA

22 21 20 19 18 17   10 9 8 7 6 5 4 3 2 1

THE INSPIRED CAREER

©2017 Jeffrey D. Hatchell, MBA

Published by:
Emerge Publishing, LLC
9521B Riverside Parkway, Suite 243
Tulsa, Oklahoma 74137
Phone: 888.407.4447
www.EmergePublishing.com

Cover Design: Christian Ophus | Emerge Publishing, LLC
Interior Design: Anita Stumbo

Library of Congress Cataloging-in-Publication Data

BISAC Category:
BUS012000 BUSINESS & ECONOMICS / Careers / General
BUS037020 BUSINESS & ECONOMICS / Careers / Job Hunting
BUS098000 BUSINESS & ECONOMICS / Knowledge Capital

Other Formats: Kindle / Nook / iBook
Hardcover ISBN: 978-1-943127-45-0
E-book ISBN: 978-1-943127-46-7

Printed in Canada.

Contents

Introduction

THIS BOOK IS STRUCTURED to allow you the flexibility to select any one chapter to read based on your need at any given moment. My recommendation is that you read it in its entirety and then use the chapters as resources. The book chapters flow and relate to each other, however, they are divided into two sections.

The first half of the book offers what I like to call "leadership inspiration." This section is comprised of five chapters that will motivate, encourage and help you perceive your career from a fresh perspective. The key to this section is the word inspire. To inspire means to breathe life into. The purpose of this first section is to build you up from the inside out, preparing your heart and mind to be more receptive to having a paradigm shift in how you think about your career.

The second half of this book provides foundational leadership strategies. The key word, foundation is defined as the underlying basis or principle for something. The concepts in these five chapters are fundamental to developing as a leader and positively impacting your career

There are coaching questions throughout both sections. Take the time to answer the questions so the ideas will come off the pages and allow you to apply them. Together, both sections combine motivational ideas with sound leadership principles. The objective is to place you in the driver's seat for your development as an individually contributing leader. This will instill a desire in you to want to be more engaged at work that will lead to you having a more fulfilling career.

OVERVIEW

There is an escalating challenge for individual contributors who work for companies and organizations of all sizes. *Forbes Magazine* published an article titled "Individual Contributors Are Forgotten Leaders: Are You Developing Them Well?" This article suggests that management is neglecting to provide needed leadership development opportunities to individual contributors. This is not only an important question for leaders to consider but even more so for individual contributors (IC) since it's directly related to their long-term career success.

This book is written primarily to provide leadership career coaching to those in organizations who are not receiving it, but desire to gain insights that can help them become more impactful and fulfilled at work. Leadership is not defined as your role or position at work. Leadership is influence. You can be at any level in any size organization and become a person of influence. This book sheds light on the essential skills to develop your career leadership beyond being competent in your current role and making goals. Making goals is critical and the entry fee for keeping your job. It's the intrinsic and soft skills that can set you apart from the bottom and middle of the corporate pyramid.

> "The most dangerous leadership myth is that leaders are born—that there is a genetic factor to leadership. That's nonsense; in fact, the opposite is true. Leaders are made rather than born." —WARREN BENNIS

What are you doing as an individual contributor to ensure you're getting the necessary leadership development to help you grow professionally? I have discovered that many ICs rely on their managers or wait for their company to spoon-feed them everything they need. What many are getting is simply compliance and technical aspects of doing their job, but not the necessary skills to become an effective leader.

I have had the privilege of coaching professionals at various corporate levels including job seekers, entry level, middle level and senior level leaders. Career coaching is needed at all levels and those who have experienced coaching have been able to learn more about themselves, in turn maximizing their potential to thrive. However, most companies only provide executive coaching to senior level executives even though there is a greater need in the middle and lower level ranks. The primary reason has to do with the investment in the person. Coaching fundamentally is a one to one practice. Companies are more inclined to make an investment in the personal development of senior level leaders as a way to help them enhance their skills for maximum performance on the job. This affords companies an ROI in senior leaders. Where as, the middle levels of organizations tend to get more generic and broader based training, if any at all. If so, it tends to be more technically related rather than focused on leadership skills. Middle level professionals also have a need to foster their skills and experiences, as they're within the talent pool for senior level opportunities.

WHO WILL BENEFIT FROM THIS BOOK?

- The person who is in corporate or seeking to get in, yet not satisfied with their current job or feels stagnant in their role.
- The person who wants to perform at another level and is not certain how to go about it.
- The corporate professional who has made it into middle management, yet fills disillusioned in their new role.
- Those who would like a fresh start and to reinvent themselves so they become a go-to person for more strategic assignments.
- The small business owner who has a great business and idea but does not have the formal leadership training for themselves or the staff
- Those who are looking for an edge and desire to redefine

him or herself to maximize their talents, experiences and strengths.

- The career professional who would like to be more fulfilled in their current role and beyond.

HOW WILL THIS BOOK BENEFIT YOU?

- This book will inspire you to explore the heart of where you are and assist you in maximizing your potential and opportunities.
- This book will help you to see your career in a more strategic manner.
- It will allow you to view your career from broader perspective rather than from your current situation.
- It will help you glean lessons from where you started and where you are today so you are better positioned for your tomorrow.
- It will help you understand how to use each experience for your ultimate good.

WHY THIS BOOK?

This is a career-coaching book that focuses on providing inspiration and leadership development.

Coaching is a term that is very popular in the corporate environment and I'll share some background information that I read in Kevin Hall's book titled *Aspire—Discovering Your Purpose Through The Power Of Words*. The word coach derives from the horse-drawn coaches that were developed in the town of Kocs during the fifteenth century. The vehicles were originally used to transport royalty, but in time they also carried valuables, mail and common passengers. Kevin states, "A coach remains something or someone who carries a valued person from where they are to where they want to be." So if you had a coach, you knew you would end up at your desired destination.

John Maxwell states in his book *The 15 Invaluable Laws of Growth* that coaches make a difference in others' lives. They help them grow, improve their potential, increase their productivity and are essential to helping people effect positive change.

This is written to be a "leadership-career coach" in book form and to help you get from where you are to where you want to be in your career.

PART 1

LEADERSHIP
INSPIRATION

"Leadership is the capacity to translate vision into reality."
—WARREN BENNIS

CHAPTER 1

The Audacity to HOPE

"Hope is a waking dream." —Aristotle

I WILL BEGIN BY DEFINING the words "audacity" and "hope." I'm sure you know what they mean but I want to amplify it for the purpose of setting up my story.

"The difference between a vision and a daydream is the audacity to act." –Steven Furtick

Audacity is defined in the dictionary as a daring spirit, resolution or confidence, venturesome. A few other words listed include shameless, boldness or insolent, heedlessness of restraints. A few synonyms for audacity include nerve, spunk, grit, and heart.

I define *hope* as confident expectation.

I like to look up common words and phrases in the dictionary to help gain deeper insights. The meaning of words in many cases change over time and tend to have new and different meanings and uses. Take the word "cool" as an example. Today cool is related to temperature as in an object being cool to the touch. It's also used to mean fine, good, nice, and okay when in the context of how something or someone is doing. Word usage in the context of a sentence also can change the meaning of the word. Like the word *audacity* can have a positive or a negative reference depending on how it's used in a sentence. For example, if I said, "That women had the audacity to reprimand her direct report publicly in front of all his peers for coming to the meeting late," rather than, "That man had the audacity to think he could actually sign that big account that's been a long time hold out."

Going to a dictionary, especially an older version helps to better understand the origin of the word. This adds illumination and an understanding of its original intent. The definition of a word or phrase can be adjusted if everyone accepts the new meaning and responds accordingly when communicating. I bring this up as a way to get us thinking about the words we choose to use and to help us think about them in a different way that will help our message. As you read about my story on the audacity of hope, I'd like you to think, contemplate and mull over the words and concepts for positive applications for you.

I created an acronym for the word HOPE as a way to leverage this powerful and important word for all of us. Having a sense of hope in the work environment is what will keep us all pursuing goals and having faith that we can achieve it. Without a sense of hope we can become discouraged when things get tough or don't go the way we desire. However, with hope you still have an expectation of a brighter future. You are looking forward to the next opportunity because of hope.

Here is the acronym for HOPE that I'd like to share:

- **H**ave a big dream
- **O**vercome obstacles
- **P**erceive the best in every situation
- **E**xpect to receive

HAVE A BIG DREAM

Most people dream and have aspirations for a brighter future but how big do we dream? How large of a goal do we set? When I went through coaching training, Coach U taught me the acronym "BHAG." It stands for *Big, Hairy, Audacious, Goal.* The idea was to ensure our goals were significant and a true stretch that when accomplished, it would make us cry out of happiness.

A big goal will push us beyond our comfort zone and cause us to become someone beyond who we are today. Henry Curtis stated, "Make your plans as fantastic as you like, because 25 years from now, they will seem mediocre. Make your plans 10 times as great as you first planned and 25 years from now you will wonder why you did not make them 50 times as great." It's relative to your vision and belief. Once you achieve a goal it gives you the confidence and momentum to make and achieve bigger goals.

MY STORY

As a kid I always wanted to work in business. I didn't know exactly what I wanted to do but I recall watching the television show called "Bewitched." I recall the husband used to go to work in a suit with a brief case. I recall he had to work with customers and do business presentations. For whatever reason, that type of job appealed to me. I also used to watch another TV show called "The Jefferson's" where the main character was George who owned dry cleaning businesses and he also wore a suit and was successful. That made me think that maybe I could run my own business.

My first job was when I was about 13. I had a paper route in the neighborhood and would deliver newspapers and collect money from my customers once a week. When I was 16, I decided to work for McDonald's since it was my favorite fast food restaurant.

At McDonald's I started working in the back flipping burgers. During those years they assigned most of the males to work in the back and would have most females on the counter taking customer orders. One day they needed help on the register and the manager asked me to come up for a quick training on it. I picked it up quickly and thoroughly enjoyed meeting customers and up-selling their order, super sizing their fries or adding an apple pie to their meal. No one taught me about cross selling, as I was not familiar with the term during those years. However, I naturally did it as an extension of my service. They could have put me on a McDonald's commercial because I was the guy with the big smile that loved McDonald's and would make you feel great for coming in my line.

One day my oldest sister Darlene came in my line and saw me in action. She later told me I should go into sales, as it seemed to fit my personality. I took it to heart and focused on business administration at Mercer County Community College and majored in marketing when I attended Howard University a few years later. While at Howard University, I had to work to help pay for my education and thought if I'm going to work, why not work for the best company possible. I decided to apply for a job with IBM as a college student. It was my way of thinking big during those years by applying at such a large Fortune 50 organization. I wowed them with my McDonald's resume and my personal accomplishments, obtained a job in the sales department working with marketing representatives, while supporting the branch manager and systems engineers.

This gave me exposure to corporate sales and an appetite for working for large corporations. I worked for IBM for about 18 months and then interned in consumer sales with Bristol Myers Squibb, working at Pitney Bowes in sales my last year of college.

After graduating from Howard University, I worked in sales roles for seven years and obtained my MBA from Nova Southeastern University in Davie, Florida. Then, I worked for an additional seven years in sales as well as sales management roles. During those years, my big hairy audacious goal was to become an entrepreneur.

As I worked over those 13 years, I would read many motivational books and listen to inspirational tapes and CD's (I used tapes during the early years). Reading and listening to motivational books inspired me to want to leverage my strengths and become an entrepreneur. After much reflection from my journal entries and discussions with personal friends and coaches, I decided to become an independent corporate trainer. This became my big goal since I was so accustomed to working in large companies in sales. Doing this would be a major stretch and a step of faith. Over a period of time, I mapped out a plan of action that included going to work for a training company to learn more about the industry, how to sell training and create training curriculum.

At this point, I had 14 years of sales and sales management experience. I was working as a sales director for American Express on Wall Street in New York. This was a childhood dream come true. All was going well and I did not have to leave Amex. However, I felt that time was ticking and if I was going to go for it, I knew there would never be a perfect time so I decided I would do it. I gave my notice and transitioned to a small training company in New York who focused primarily on business communications skills training. My job was to sell the services to large companies and deliver the training that I sold. They also took me through an in depth training to certify me in their curriculum. I was getting all the experience I desired with this firm. My plan was to stay there to learn all I could and then launch out on my own.

But … *I was fired!*

After working for this training company for a year, I was doing okay with the sales part but was enjoying the training part of the job. They were acquired by a larger holding company and they hired a new president to run the company. One day I came to work and my immediate leader who was a vice president asked me to come into his office. As I walked in, I noticed the new president of the company came in right behind me and closed the door. The VP started to speak to me about how the company was having a challenging year meeting its financial goals and I noticed an envelope in the president's hand with my name on it. The VP kept speaking but my mind was racing—thinking they might be in the process of firing me. When I mentally tuned back to what my VP was saying I heard the words, "economic cut backs and they would have to let me go." I was shocked and couldn't believe that I could work for all these major Fortune 100 companies and do well and go for my, "big, hairy, audacious goal" and get fired!? I had an attitude and said to myself, *How dare they fire me. Don't they know who I am?* It took a while for it to sink in that I was actually fired while in the process of pursuing my big dream.

OVERCOME OBSTACLES

The letter "O" in the HOPE acronym is for *overcome obstacles.* This experience could have devastated me. I could have decided to not pursue any big, hairy, audacious, goals for reasons such as this. However, I had to use this as a learning experience to help me go beyond this situation. Have you ever been fired? If so, I'm sure you can appreciate going through the emotional challenges that comes along with getting fired. For those of you who were never let go, learning from an experience is more valuable than going through an experience. John Maxwell wrote, *"Experience alone does not add value to life. It's not necessarily experience that is valuable; it's the insight people gain because of their experience."* Getting fired did not stop my goal from happening. At the time, I felt it was simply a delay because shortly after, I moved to California and noticed there was a significant difference in the cost of living. As a result, I decided to return to the traditional corporate environment and within two months I obtained a job as a Vice President with Wells Fargo leading a sales team.

I had to overcome the mental anguish of being fired after I decided to go for my goal again. My obstacle to overcome was the fear of going for it again and it not working out. Transitioning careers to the training industry was just the first step of my long-term strategy in becoming an independent corporate trainer. Getting fired at that point was like taking years and effort to prepare to become a professional basketball player and getting cut at the high school level. This is what happened to Michael Jordan, the famous professional NBA player who is a Hall of Famer, five-time MVP award winner and six-time NBA team champion title holder. However, when he was in the tenth grade he did not make the varsity team and he was devastated. I learned that this made Michael Jordan work harder to become better to ensure he would never be cut again. This obstacle pushed him to work harder at perfecting his game. Michael Jordan is quoted as stating on his website, "I think that not making the varsity team drove me to really work at my game, and also taught me that if you set goals, and work hard to achieve them—the hard work can pay off." During the off-season, he practiced every aspect of the basketball game and improved well beyond the average player. Another favorite quote from Jordan related to overcoming obstacles is:

"Obstacles don't have to stop you. If you run into a wall, don't turn around and give up. Figure out how to climb it, go through it, or work around it."

We all go through obstacles and I'm certain everyone reading this has many examples. The goal is in overcoming them. As the Reverend Jesse Jackson says, "Keep hope alive." I kept the goal alive through my journaling while continuing to feed on inspiring books that helped to stir up the desire and fan the flames in me. Otherwise, after going through a challenge such as getting fired in the early stages, it could have easily led to that passionate flame flickering out.

I went back into traditional corporate but still had the desire for entrepreneurship so while working full time I started taking classes at Coach U to obtain my coaching certification. My plan was still to become a corporate trainer and I decided I would add coaching to my offerings. Going through Coach U allowed me to learn more about the training industry and meet others who had a similar desire. I was able to collaborate with others and learn from them about best practices. I recall hearing about an article in *Business Week* during that time that more people were becoming coaches and the average annual income for coaches was about 10% of what I desired. It was disappointing for me as my goal was to be able to generate more than enough so I could do it full time instead of working a traditional full time job.

It made me want to learn what it would take to generate over six-figures so I sought out coaches who were doing it. I began with my Coach U instructors and then I got involved in other organizations to meet other, more successful coaches. This would later pay off.

PERCEIVE **THE BEST**

One of the best things I learned to do in an effort to overcome obstacles and challenges was to ***perceive*** the best in everything. I learned to find the good in every situation and to see it as working for my ultimate good. It is being an optimist.

There's a story I heard about two brothers. One became a doctor and the other was in jail for selling illegal drugs. They were both interviewed and asked the same question by a reporter: "*What do you attribute to you being where you are today?*" The son who was in jail for selling drugs responded to the question by sharing that his mom died when he was young and his father was abusive, an alcoholic, on drugs, and in and out of jail on a regular basis. He stated that based on this background he felt it was inevitable for him to end up like his father. The other son who became a doctor responded to the question by sharing that his mom died when he was young and his father was abusive, an alcoholic, on drugs, and in and out of jail on a regular basis. He stated that based on this background he knew he would have to do the opposite of his father so he would not end up in jail like him.

Two brothers raised by the same parents in the same household with two very different outcomes. They experienced the same things growing up; however, they *perceived* it differently. One perceived it as a helpless situation and the other saw it as an opportunity to change his future. How do you perceive things that happen to you or in your life? We all have and will have obstacles and challenges. However, it's how we see and internalize them that can make a difference for us whether good or bad. Are you an optimist or a pessimist? The traditional test question is the glass half full or is it half empty? There is no wrong answer; it all depends on how you choose to see it.

In his book *The 7 Habits of Highly Effective People,* Stephen Covey defines paradigm shift as the way an individual perceives, understands and interprets the surrounding world. The shift is making a sudden change in how we see our situation.

The following illustration is a young lady with a black shawl, a necklace, curly black hair and a large hat with a feather in the front. Her head is turned in the other direction so you can only see her side profile. Or, is it a picture of an older woman with a large nose and chin, glancing down with a bag under her left eye and a fur coat? It's both an older women and a younger lady but it might take you a while to see both women in the picture. For some it comes easily and for others it takes time or might have to be pointed out for them to see. It all depends on your perspective.

Illustration Credit: W.E. Hill

Helen Keller was the first deaf and blind person to graduate with a bachelor's degree. She was a writer, a teacher and a political activist. She was interviewed and asked a question by an interviewer, "What could be worse than being blind?" She responded and said:

"The only thing worse than being blind is having sight and no vision."

Helen Keller is known to be the ultimate optimist in spite of being blind and deaf. She chose to focus on the good and to make the most of her circumstance. Let her be an example and illustration of willingness to adjust your perspective to see things through an optimistic lens. It's easy to take the obvious path of responding to our natural circumstances but it takes a conscious effort and a choice to see things differently regardless of the obstacles.

I learned to perceive the best in my current situation. I had a job coaching and leading others as a Vice President with a major Fortune 100 company and I was able to go through a great coaching program with Corporate Coach U to begin my coaching business on the side. I started to see that my job and the coaching program were both great opportunities that helped to prepare me for my ultimate goal. As I began to see things from this positive perspective it helped me to fully leverage my current situation and to see opportunities that I previously would not have noticed. I also began to perceive the job I lost working for the training company as an experience that I could still leverage. I learned to see the good from that experience. I recalled during that one-year time I went through extensive training and did become a certified presentation skills instructor. I also learned how to sell training to Fortune 500 companies and did close several deals for the training firm. I learned how to conduct group training, one-on-one training and worked with people in various industries, roles and levels.

As I began to consider all the good things I was able to take a way from the experience it helped me to feel better about myself. Many can go through a situation where they were focused on a big goal and ended up losing their job. It can naturally cause a person to become discouraged which could lead to depression if they consider seeing things from a negative perspective. Rather, we have to make a conscious effort to choose to learn from the situation and find the good that you can take from the experience. It took time for me to figure out that it was more beneficial for me to make an effort to find and focus on the good of what I initially thought was an unfortunate situation.

After being fired, I initially focused on all of the negative things of the situation and I felt like a victim: "How dare they fire me! Don't they know who I am?" Those were some of my first thoughts. I've worked for major Fortune 500 companies and have been promoted and done well. I also have my MBA and deserve to be running things at the company versus getting fired. I also focused on thoughts of, now what am I going to do. They gave me a small severance, but I was concerned about what would happen when that ran out. How challenging and how long would it take for me to get another job to replace that income, etc? The more I focused on the negative the more I became a victim trapped in a circumstance of having been fired and needing to get another job, quickly.

Victor Frankl wrote a book titled *Man's Search for Meaning*. This was based on his experience as a concentration camp inmate during the Second World War. He observed that those who survived the longest in the concentration camps were not those who were the strongest physically but those who mentally took control over their environment. Frankl felt that it was by connecting to such a sense of purpose that Holocaust survivors were able to make it through such a challenging time. Even in the worst imaginable circumstances, Frankl holds firm to the belief that man's spirit can rise above his surroundings. He wrote:

"When we are no longer able to change a situation, we are challenged to change ourselves."

This book inspired me to learn and find purpose or meaning out of bad situations. This gave me a sense of hope and optimism to look for next steps and believe that better things were in store for me.

Years ago, I recall seeing movies about conspiracy theories and many people making comments about occurrences that happened in their life being part of a bigger plot by the government or some large external organization. Almost as if external forces or people were setting the stage for things to happen that would negatively impact a group of people. Conspiracy theories have been related to a variety of things including past assassinations or deaths of famous people, technology, wars, stock market fluctuations, and many others. However, I only recall hearing of conspiracy theories with some type of negative implication.

When I was hearing things like this, I decided to believe in conspiracy theories that had positive implications. So whenever something would happen to me whether good or not, my mind-set was this is working out for my ultimate good. I choose to believe the scripture (Romans 8:28) that states, "and we know that all things work together for good for those who love God and are called according to His purpose." I choose to believe this as my conspiracy theory. That regardless of what happens, it will all work out for my good. Thomas Edison is known to have said:

> "I have not failed, I just found 10,000 ways
> that won't work."

This statement is related to the amount of times he tried to invent the light bulb. He could have given up at his first few attempts but instead of viewing experiments that did not work as failures he viewed them as learning experiences. How many of us can relate to such a statement concerning our so-called failures? To see getting fired, not getting the promotion, not getting the job that we thought was a perfect fit, not closing the big sale or missing the anticipated results of a project as part of a bigger picture. Consider it part of the process to fulfilling your ultimate goal. Yet, being willing to continue to pursue your endeavor and viewing the setbacks in a positive light.

I'd like to encourage you to make a conscious decision to see things that happen in your life from that perspective. I have been through getting fired, not getting a desired job or promotion but have learned to believe that there is something better that will work out in my favor. This attitude helps us to view circumstances and challenges related to our career as a part of the process to get us where we really want to be.

EXPECT TO RECEIVE

Expect is a synonym for the words hope, anticipate and to look for something. Having a positive expectation about your future is essential in giving us purpose for our daily activities. Expectation can be towards something positive or negative. In this section, I'm focusing on the positive. The things that encourage and excite us to be, do, or have.

"Hope deferred makes the heart sick, but a dream fulfilled is a tree of life." —PROVERBS 13:12

I remember when I was a kid on Christmas Eve how excited I was to open my presents under the tree. I wanted to try to figure out what my gifts were and I'd sometimes try to find them to get some indication. I couldn't fall asleep as I was hoping I would receive certain ones that I talked about most. I'd see myself playing with them and thinking how fun it would be to have them in a few hours. I was excited because I was looking forward to receiving something I wanted and believed I would get. The next morning when it was time to open the gifts I would quickly rip off the wrapping paper and jump for joy for my gifts. In some cases I received the gifts I wanted and in other cases I would get a few of my desired gifts. Regardless, I would be happy playing with my new gifts all day long and it always brought great experiences. Part of the enjoyment of getting Christmas presents is the positive expectation of receiving.

Carrying this attitude as it relates to expecting can go a long way in helping us to appreciate and esteem the things we receive. Having the positive anticipation can increase the enjoyment and the value of the moment of reception. Women go through a lot before experiencing the fulfilling joy of delivering a child. However, when they hear the first cry or get to hold their baby for the first time, their joy becomes full. Partly, because of the expectation and partly to see that everything worked out, both of which provide a sense of fulfillment. Using this approach in our career can help us better appreciate the process of receiving.

Think about things in your life that you have been expecting. In most cases when we are expecting something we prepare for it and begin to look for it. Think about when you're expecting a special friend or relative to come visit you at your residence. You may prepare your place by cleaning and straightening up. You may prepare a meal or make sure you have beverages in your fridge. After a while you may begin to look for their arrival by looking out the window or checking your phone for any updates. We take these steps of preparation when we believe we will receive what we expect. I suggest we leverage this same process for our goals. Do your part to prepare, be on the look out for opportunities, support and innovative ideas. Have your antenna up when speaking to others, reading, in meetings or even watching movies. All these things can help lead to a great fulfillment of your goals.

Back to my story ...

After I was let go from the training company and back in corporate and taking coaching classes, I began to expect things to work out for me. Based on making a shift in my perspective of my situation, I felt that I was doing all I knew. I was preparing for the fulfillment of my ultimate goal. As I was taking the coaching classes I would constantly ask other coaches for key success factors. I began signing up with other coaches who were doing workshops, seminars and training sessions. I wanted to learn all I could to become a successful coach and trainer. I was working hard on myself and on my job that led to me having a reason to expect it to go well. I've learned that *it's one thing to hope for things to work out and it's another thing to do my best in setting myself up for success.*

I began looking and asking for opportunities. I got to a point where I felt that I was well equipped and needed to take action on my belief that my big hairy audacious goal would become a reality. Based on my experience of working in corporate for years, I used to feel that I was always in a position of preparing myself for something. I would analyze reports, review marketing data and learn best practices from others. I'd do these things in preparation for the next position, project or assignment. I also observed in myself and others that we could continue to remain in a circle of analyzing and preparing ourselves. I later learned the importance of not only preparing myself but also being willing to take action, make mistakes and consider those experiences part of the learning and preparation process. I've learned the importance of taking some type of step toward the fulfillment of my goal and expecting results.

As a result of my expectations, I started telling everyone I knew that I was taking coaching classes with the goal of doing it full time. My first paying coaching client was a friend who was running an executive recruiting firm. We went to undergrad together at Howard University and he obtained a Harvard MBA. He thoroughly enjoyed the results from our coaching sessions and began recommending me to his clients and friends. This led to getting other clients from other coaches who were inviting me to conferences to coach with them. I became very busy as I was still working a full time job as a VP with Wells Fargo, leading a team of ten sales people. I was coaching late nights over the phone, weekends and every other time I could find. I was expecting the coaching business to grow. In an effort to grow my motivational speaking and leadership workshop opportunities, I began doing lunch and learn sessions for local employee resource groups of companies in the Bay area. This led to me obtaining corporate clients and generating more through my business than my full time corporate job. This allowed me to leave the safety net of my corporate job and launch out into the wild of entrepreneurship on a full time basis. My hobby turned into my occupation and I was just as happy on the day I fulfilled my big, hairy, audacious goal as I was as a kid on Christmas morning.

Having a big dream of running my own training company was fulfilled in April 2006. This was a result of me *having* a big goal, *overcoming* obstacles of getting fired, *perceiving* the best of my situation and *expecting* my dream to become my reality. My goal in sharing this example is to inspire you to use the HOPE acronym to live your dreams as well.

HOPE IS RECYCLABLE

However, this story does not end in the typical fairy tale manner of "… and they lived happily ever after …" In 2008, the U.S. economy began to take a turn for the worse and I went through a type of economic depression. There was a run on money in the financial sector, many companies began to close, the stock market lost significant value, the real estate market crashed and many foreclosures took place. Most began to lose money on their retirement accounts. It was a tough time for most if not all businesses, large and small. Some say it was worse than what was considered the great depression of the early 1900s and there were books written and documentaries made that highlighted how close the U.S. financial institutions were to a financial collapse than the average person knew. Books like *Too Big to Fail: The Inside Story of How Wall Street* and *Washington Fought to Save the Financial System—and Themselves* by Andrew Ross Sorkin outlined that period of time was the most tumultuous period in America's financial history.

In 2009, this economic decline continued to negatively impact businesses and ultimately showed up at my doorstep. My large clients began to inform me they could not continue to honor our contract and needed to cancel it despite our written legal agreement. I was hearing this or variations like this from almost all of my large corporate clients. I went from being on retainers with large organizations to getting one-off opportunities with no guarantee of getting follow-up work. I had personal clients who were also impacted and were having challenges paying their mortgage and needed to cease paying me as their coach.

I was living my dream and now my fairy tale story that turned into reality was beginning to fall apart. I was still getting business and had clients, however, it was not enough to sustain my lifestyle at the time. After being challenged financially and personally, I was at a crossroads and had to make a decision about continuing my efforts to revive my business or make a decision to return to the corporate environment as an employee. I chose the latter as it appeared to be the safe and more logical choice for me. Therefore, I updated my resume and began by informing my clients of my intention to return to corporate full time. I had several senior level contacts at American Express who were gracious and allowed me to return in a director level position that was at the same level I had resigned from six years prior.

This experience reminded me that "life" happens. I know others who started similar businesses and were able to make it through the tough season. However, that's not my story and I'm okay with how my situation is unique. As I have shared this story, many informed me they could relate and have had similar experiences. This is where having the "Audacity to HOPE" comes into play for me again. I am just recycling the HOPE process and believe that this is working out for my ultimate good and will inspire many others to keep HOPE alive.

MUHAMMAD ALI – A CHAMPION AND EXAMPLE OF HOPE

The late Muhammad Ali was a great professional boxer and considered by many to be one of the best boxers in history. He's also known as "The Champ." I had an opportunity to meet him twice in my life. The first was when I was a kid and went on a trip to his training camp in the hills of Pennsylvania. The second was as an adult on a business trip. I saw him in a hotel lobby in Salt Lake City, Utah, shook his hand and had a conversation with him where he let myself and my co-workers know that he still "has it." I am a big fan and consider him a champion of the people and a great example of consistently living out my Audacity to HOPE acronym.

I read his bio and learned that Cassius Clay, Jr.—during his early years before changing his name—had the big dream of becoming the heavy weight champion of the world when he was in high school in Louisville, Kentucky. He started boxing as a teenager and always felt that he was fast and pretty. He has always been known to speak out what he wanted and his expectations about winning fights. He would also state what he would do to his opponent's months before he got into a ring with them.

Muhammad Ali had many famous fights and victories throughout his boxing career. I will highlight his fight against Joe Frazier as an example of leveraging the Audacity of HOPE.

In April 1967, Ali was drafted in the U.S. Army and refused to go because of his religious beliefs at the time. As a result, he was arrested and his boxing license was revoked. He was the reigning champion at the time because he had beaten Sunny Liston who had the belt. Ali risked all and created a big obstacle to overcome. He was not able to fight for over three years during the prime years for a boxer. He risked going to jail and not being able to box again.

When Ali's boxing license was reinstated in 1970, he returned to the ring, fought and knocked out Jerry Quarry. This opened a door for Ali to fight Joe Frazier, the reigning champion at the time. Frazier agreed to give him an opportunity to fight for the heavy weight championship belt.

This was a chance for Ali to regain the championship title that was his big dream. However, after their fight Joe Frazier knocked Ali down in the last round even though Ali got back on his feet. Ali lost his big opportunity in what was considered the fight of the century.

Afterwards, Ali was interviewed about the fight and asked by a reporter what happened when he was knocked out. Ali responded that he was not knocked out or down and would show everyone what he would do in the rematch. Ali refused to acknowledge the knock down and kept his focus on what he would do to Frazier in the next fight. This is a great example of perceiving the best in every situation. He didn't see it as a loss but part of the process.

After Ali lost the first fight with Frazier, he worked on improving his skills and being in better physical shape. He was preparing to win because he expected to win the next fight. As a result, Ali won the second fight and regained his championship title. He gave Frazier a rematch that made it their third fight and Ali won again, securing his championship position.

Muhammad Ali had a big dream of being the heavy weight-boxing champion of the world. He overcame the obstacles of losing his boxing license and he perceived the best in spite of being knocked out. Finally, Ali expected to beat Frazier during his second and third fights and demonstrated it.

COACHING QUESTIONS

1. Have a big dream — what's your big dream?
2. What obstacles do you need to overcome?
3. What do you perceive that's good in your situation?
4. What are you expecting and what are you doing to prepare yourself to receive?

CHAPTER 2

Time Is Ticking!

"Everything on earth has its own time and its own season."
—Ecclesiastes 3:1

T HE CLICHÉ IS TRUE—*time is running out.* I understand there are 24 hours a day, 7 days a week, 365 days a year. However, the obvious is not always taken literally or as seriously as it should be. The goal of this chapter is to be a wake-up call for us to become more conscious of the time factor. I want us to better grasp how time can be elusive if we are not careful to fully leverage this precious resource.

USA Today had an article in October 2014 that referenced a new report on mortality in the USA from the Centers for Disease Control and Prevention's National Center for Health Statistics.

It states that life expectancy in the USA rose in 2012 to 78.8 from 78.7 in 2011. It detailed that life expectancy for females is 81.2 years and for males, 76.4 years. Worldwide, the average life expectancy at birth was 71 years (73.2 for females and 68.5 for males) over the period 2010–2013 according to United Nations World Population Prospects.

The following is an exercise that I'd like you to take the time *(pun intended)* to complete. It will help to illuminate that time is ticking. Feel free to use your phone calculator.

1. Type in your current age and multiply by 365. I am 49 at the time of this writing so the calculation is 49×365=17,885. This provides you with your age in days.

2. Now take that number and subtract it from 28,835, the average life span in the USA of 79 multiplied by 365. The equation is now 28,835−17,520=10,950.

The equation yields the total life expectancy in days by subtracting our current age in days to come up with a general idea of how many days we have left if we live to the average age of 79. In this example, I would have 10,950 days remaining to do everything I planned to do because time is running out.

> How many days do you have remaining and
> what are you going to do with it?

I'm sure you're like me in doing everything you know to exceed the life span average so you will have more days. However, this paints a picture of letting us know our time is limited. I want to magnify this point to help create some urgency for us in living the life we desire by fulfilling our goals and dreams.

When you see an obituary they normally have the person's age displayed as the date they were born and then a dash with the date they died (i.e., 1930–2009). The question is:

What are you going to do with your dash?

I recognize some of this may sound a little morbid but it's a reality check to help wake us up to the fact that time is indeed ticking. Your dash represents what you did with the time you were allotted and since you're reading this it let's us know we still have time but not a lot of it.

Another helpful exercise in this regard is to write your obituary. Think about people representing different areas of your life and what they would say about you. Think about what you would prefer them to say about you when you're gone. The goal is to bridge the gap if one exists on what you would like said versus what would currently be stated. The thought is to be whom you wish to be perceived so others don't have to exaggerate the truth or misrepresent you at your funeral to try to appease those in attendance.

Think about all the roles you play and hats you wear. As I think about my life some of the following roles come to mind— father, stepfather, husband, brother, uncle, nephew, coach, teacher, manager, trainer, elder, son, director, vice president, employee, co-worker, president, or student. I could go on and on and I'm sure you can too. However, let's limit it to our top five general roles such as:

1. Spouse
2. Parent
3. Friend
4. Coworker (including if you were the boss, subordinate or colleague)
5. Community involvement (including role in any variation of church, non-profit organizations, athletic leagues, gyms, etc.)

If you had one person speak at your funeral representing each of your primary areas, what would you like them to say? The following are a few areas of consideration and for the purpose of this exercise, please limit it to your top five:

- Immediate family
- Extended family
- Friends
- Work/business life/professional life
- Community life

The first part of this exercise is to think about what one person representing each group would honestly say about you if you just died. The second part is to think about what you would want them to say if you died at an old age.

Capture all of what comes to mind in writing in a notebook or your journal (we will discuss journaling in the chapter on goal setting works). After writing your initial thoughts take some time to read it over and update as necessary. If you give it some time, I'm sure you will be enlightened and hopefully encouraged to make changes as necessary to live out the life you desire. The objective is for you to design your life by becoming the person you want to be in all the areas of your life.

After you have written what you want people in those buckets to say about you, write out what you will do differently. If you feel like you're doing everything you'd want everyone to say, then capture what you can do to enhance it.

The dash in between your birth and death represents your legacy. What impact are we making and how have we or are we making a difference with our time. I want to share a true story with you on the impact of seeing our own obituary.

One morning in 1888 Alfred Noble, the inventor of dynamite, awoke to read his own obituary. The obituary was printed as a result of a simple journalistic error. You see, it was Alfred's brother that had died and the reporter carelessly reported the death of the wrong brother.

Any man would be disturbed under the circumstances, but to Alfred the shock was overwhelming because he saw himself as the world saw him—the "Dynamite King," the great industrialist who had made an immense fortune from explosives. This, as far as the general public was concerned, was the entire purpose of Alfred's life. None of his true intentions to break down the barriers that separated men and ideas for peace were recognized or given serious consideration. He was simply a merchant of death. And for that alone he would be remembered.

As he read the obituary with horror, he resolved to make clear to the world the true meaning and purpose of his life. This could be done through the final disposition of his fortune. His last will and testament would be the expression of his life's ideals and ultimately would be why we would remember him. The result was the most valuable of prizes given to those who had done the most for the cause of world peace. It is called today the "Nobel Peace Prize."

I hope you see the value in completing your obituary so you can truly make a difference in life that you believe you were created to fulfill.

The late Myles Munroe, a leadership expert, made the following comments:

"The wealthiest places in the world are not gold mines, oil fields, diamond mines or banks. The wealthiest place is the cemetery. There lies companies that were never started, masterpieces that were never painted … In the cemetery there is buried the greatest treasure of untapped potential. There is a treasure within you that must come out. Don't go to the grave with your treasure still within you."

Vince Lombardi the famous football coach of the Green Bay Packers in the 1960s is known for saying, *We didn't lose the game, we just ran out of time.* He stated this at the end of a game in which they lost. This makes me think about how in many professional sports like basketball, football and soccer that winning is based on where we are at a specific time. It's the team with the most points at the end of regulation time that is considered the winner. However, as I grew up playing on the playground with my friends, we based the winner on who was first to get to a pre-determined amount of points. However, in professional sports it's all based on time. One of the things that makes a game exciting and in some cases anxiety driven is due to the change in score as you watch the time tick away. The more time that comes off the clock the more intense especially with a close game.

In school when taking tests, it's normally based on a limited amount of time. Taking the subject of math, is all about problem solving. The challenge and opportunity is being able to solve the problems in the most efficient or time effective manner. Many could figure out a math problem if you give them as much time as they need. However, the difference makers are usually those who are able to figure it out in the shortest amount of time.

In business, things are measured based on how much is generated typically based on monthly, quarterly and annual goals. My background is working in sales roles. I always had annual goals. There's an old saying in sales: "What have you done for me lately?" and "You're only as good as your last sale." Meaning, if you had a great year last year, it's forgotten as soon as you start the new sales period. That was then—this is now.

All these examples are to help show that time is moving in all areas of our lives. It's about making the most of the time since it's limited. We may not know exactly how much time we have remaining so it should encourage all of us to live as if it's limited.

Most kids have an attitude of going for everything and not being concerned about getting hurt. As we get older we can become more conservative and cautious in our activities. We start to understand that we are not invincible but we are fragile and able to be hurt. However, we can make the most of the time we have by going for our goals and choosing to live our best by being our best self.

SEASONALITY OF A CAREER

Back in the day, a career goal would be to get a job with a great company and work there until retirement. Promotions would come primarily based on tenure with the company. Most looked forward to staying long enough to get to the next level. Today, things are different. The average person stays at each of their jobs for 4.6 years, according to the Bureau of Labor Statistics in 2014. However, the study stated the expected tenure of the work-force's youngest employees is about half of the average today. According to a Forbes article, it stated that job-hopping is the new normal for millennials. They have learned to drive career advancement through constant change.

Careers are not lineal. Meaning, people normally do not go in a direct line straight up the corporate ladder. In my experience, people take a lot of detours. A typical career progression could include regression and many laterals prior to ascending up. In addition, many go through different stages not only in level but also in their personal lives while on the job which impacts their emotional intelligence. Emotional Intelligence is the

Career Progression

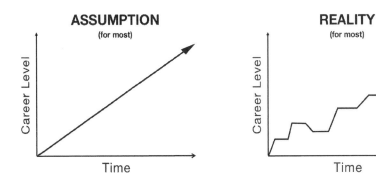

ability to recognize one's own and other people's emotions, to discriminate between different feelings and label them appropriately, and to use emotional information to guide thinking and behavior. It impacts how they feel about what they do and their performance as well as passion. I like to relate it to the natural seasons of nature.

We generally have four seasons, depending on the part of the world or country in which you live—winter, spring, summer and fall. There are different environmental factors and outcomes for each season.

SPRING

Spring is a transition time of refreshing, regrowth and renewal. It's a time of year when the weather begins to be warmer and rain showers kick in. It's a time of planting and preparation. Spring represents new beginnings and fresh starts. Naturally speaking, it comes right after winter and most are excited about the transition.

We leverage daylight savings time for more daylight by springing our clocks forward. Many look forward to spring cleaning and putting away the winter sweaters and wool coats. It's the season for homes to begin to go on the market. Many look forward to doing more outdoor activities and the ability to take advantage of the warmer climate.

Relating it to work is like when first starting a new job or position. During the honeymoon phase, everything seems fresh. New hires tend to be eager to go the extra mile . When most first begin they are so excited, they are glad to come in early and stay late. They will do whatever they can to reach out to everyone on the team. They schedule lunch and coffee meetings with peers to assess the business and to learn best practices. Spring rain coming down can be representative of the people leaders providing positive affirmations for initial efforts since the rain and sun are necessary factors that spurs growth. The positive feedback and comments help to feed initial excitement and drives new hires to want to thrive in their new environment.

When I was a kid I used to say, "April showers bring May flowers." Part of rehearsing the rhyme was a reminder to be patient during the rainy spring season knowing that it's going to end in a matter of time. The benefits of the spring rain and sun have beautiful outcomes such as flowers and other aesthetic forms of nature.

Since spring comes right after winter, it's like breaking a long fast. Springtime represents being able to enjoy what's available during this season. However, spring starts at the end of March, typically followed by rain in April and nice sunshine and modest temperatures in May.

Understanding that being in a spring season in a career is when you've come out of a tough time and now things are transitioning to be in your favor. It places you in a position of enjoying the change. Recognize when you're in this season and learn to appreciate the rain knowing you are about to blossom in your work environment. Spring season in a career provides an opportunity to leverage change and make the most of it because it's temporary.

SUMMER

Summer season is representative of long days and short nights. The weather is at its warmest of the year and people spend a lot of time outdoors and participating in outdoor activities.

The famous actor Will Smith sang a rap song about summer and here are some of the lyrics:

Summertime

School is out and it's a sort of a buzz. But back then I didn't
really know what it was. But now I see what have of this.
The way that people respond to summer madness.
The weather is hot and girls are dressin' less. And checkin'

out the fellas to tell 'em who's best. Ridin' around in your jeep or your Benzos. Or in your Nissan sittin' on Lorenzo's. Back in Philly we be out in the park. A place called the plateau is where everybody goes. Guys out huntin' and girls doin' likewise. Honkin' at the honey in front of you with the light eyes. She turn around to see what you beepin' at. It's like the summer's a natural aphrodisiac. And with a pen and pad, I compose this rhyme. To hit you and get you equipped for the summertime.

Summer, summer, summertime. Time to sit back and unwind.
Summer, summer, summertime. Time to sit back and unwind.

It's late in the day and I ain't been on the court yet. Hustle to the mall to get me a short set. Yeah, I got on sneaks but I need a new pair. 'Cause basketball courts in the summer got girls there. The temperature's about 88. Hop in the water plug just for old times sake. Creak to ya crib, change your clothes once more. 'Cause you're invited to a barbecue that's startin' at 4. Sittin' with your friends 'cause y'all reminisce. About the days growin' up and the first person you kiss. And as I think back, makes me wonder how. The smell from a grill could spark up nostalgia. All the kids playin' out front, little boys messin' 'round. With the girls playin' double-dutch. While the DJ's spinnin' a tune as the old folks. Dance at your family reunion. Then six 'o clock rolls around. You just finished wipin' your car down. It's time to cruise, so you head to. The summertime hangout, it looks like a car show. Everybody come lookin' real fine. Fresh from the barbershop or fly from the beauty salon. Every moment frontin' and maxin' Chillin' in the car they spent all day waxin'. Leanin' to the side but you can't speed through. Two miles an hour so, everybody sees you. There's an air of love and of happiness and this is the Fresh Prince's new definition of summer madness.

Summer, summer, summertime. Time to sit back and unwind.
Summer, summer, summertime. Time to sit back and unwind.

–Songwriters MAHONE, LAMAR/FINGERS/TAYLOR,
ALTON DAMERON/SMITH, CLAYDES

This song highlights many of the representations of summer activities, especially for young singles. Many tend to do things differently to take advantage of the warm temperatures and long days. It can be a time for vacations, weekend get-a-ways and connecting with friends and family.

In the work environment a summer season can represent a time of enjoyment. It can be a time when profits are high, business is strong and the future of the company looks bright as people celebrate their accomplishments. Many companies have national meetings where they bring groups together for rewards and recognition. This season for companies can be representative of a time for retreats, team building activities and off-sites. It's worthwhile to recognize this season in your career and to make the most of it. It's a time to enjoy the moment knowing that it's seasonal and subject to change. This is where being a realist can be helpful. However, it's also important to learn to live in the moment and to make the best of this time.

Many industries and market segments of businesses are cyclical. Retail businesses tend to have a high percentage of their sales during the Christmas and holiday season. Construction tends to pick up in the spring and summer months. CPAs tend to do well in the spring due to taxes needing to be filed. There are times in every organization where things may be busier than normal due to the seasonality of their business. Know what season you're in and be prepared for transitions.

FALL/AUTUMN

The fall and autumn season is also known in farming as the harvest season. It's a time when farmers get to reap from all of the seeds they've sown. It's when they get to benefit from the fruits of their labor. In the US during this season is when we have Halloween and Thanksgiving holiday. The weather is starting to transition from being hot to cooling off in the evenings. We move our clock back to standard time and the daytime is shorter. Leaves on trees begin to change colors and can be a beautiful sight in many parts of the country like the New England states. Each season has benefits and like the word season implies, it's temporary.

The Fall season is when many intentionally prepare for what's to come. Taking advantage of the season of plenty by storing and saving for when things will change. Ants are a great example of this concept. In most of the homes I've owned, no matter how new or old the house, primarily during the summer months, I'd see ants. The ants would be going out looking for food and bring it back to their nest to store it for a later time. Ants are instinctively preparing for a season when they will be hibernating and will have plenty to carry them through the wet and cold seasons or times of lack for them.

In our careers, this season may represent a time of us getting recognition for our efforts. It's a time when we are getting bonuses, stock options, raises and other incentives from our efforts. This is the season when we are closing large sales deals, successfully completing projects, exceeding goals and executing initiatives that's been in the works for some time.

Similar to the ant analogy it's also a great opportunity to capture your accomplishments and feelings in your journal. (More about journaling in Chapter 10, goal setting works!) It can come in handy to be able to review all these great things happening while you are in your winter season. Remembering the good times, the recognition and the process you took to get the promotion, raise or great review will keep you encouraged as needed.

The important thing to remember is that the good, bad and ugly are all subject to change. We should not make permanent decisions based on a temporary situation. Keeping this in mind can support decision making for long-term impact.

WINTER

The fourth major season is winter. It's a time of colder weather, shorter days, snow or rain depending on where you live. We typically adjust our dress to the weather with sweaters, boots, hats and gloves. Our diet tends to adjust to more comfort foods and hot meals like soup, stews, roasts and ciders. We proactively make many changes for the difference in season so we can manage what's happening more effectively.

In business, our winter season can be a time of making adjustments to a new environment such as some type of organizational change. Our winter season at work can be a time when we are not doing as well or a time of not enjoying our position. It can be a time of getting a new leader that you don't care for and is making your job tougher than necessary. It's typically something going on at work that is not as pleasing to you and you have to work through it. Understanding it's a winter season and believing that spring will come soon can be encouraging.

I've been assigned to coach people who I considered to be in their winter season. One person I recall coaching was at a major Fortune 50 company. Senior leadership brought me in as a last ditch effort to help him improve his interpersonal skills. He was a great employee with high credentials, an Ivy League education and a great background in leading large teams but many complained about his interpersonal skills. As a result, they took away all of his direct reports and assigned me to coach him. For the purpose of this example, I'll call him Al.

Al was a tenured employee with experience as a leader. He totally understood why they assigned me to work with him. He was disappointed that things in his career had come to this point. However, after asking many questions to assess the situation from his vantage point, I learned that Al was simply in a winter season of his career. I shared with Al that this situation could be considered temporary and it was up to him to turn this into a spring season. He understood and was willing to go through the process. The beginning was for Al to recognize what season he was in and to instill in him that it was subject to change based on his desire to adjust.

Al thought through the situation and we discussed various options that included looking for other roles externally. I challenged Al to not resign but to be willing to step up to the plate and make the necessary tweaks to rebound. I didn't want him to extend this winter season by not learning the potential leadership lesson by simply going to another company. I've seen many people leave a challenging situation only to find themselves in the same situation down the road at another organization. A lesson not learned will be repeated. My goal was to coach Al to learn the necessary lessons so he would not have to experience this situation again.

After Al bought into the idea that this was a temporary situation that he had the control to change, I had him complete a 360 assessment. I had direct conversations with everyone he connects with regularly at work to get their input. He took the feedback and we went to work on adjusting the core issues and

Al changed his style to become more approachable and social. After a few months he took the 360 again and the results were astoundingly positive. He worked on changing his outcome and as a result was able to get out of his winter season and ultimately took on new responsibilities and led a team again.

In many cases, a winter season in a company will naturally change given enough time. It can organically happen due to the economy improving, regulatory changes and other external factors. In other cases like with Al, there are things we can do to change the season of our career. In an effort to coach you to navigate through the uncharted waters of corporate, it can be beneficial to think about the natural seasons.

Consider how every year we expect to go through spring, summer, fall/autumn and winter. It's pretty much guaranteed that we will go through each season. The key is that we go through the season and prepare accordingly. When we are in expectation of each of the seasons it's not so much a surprise that can prevent us from making long-term decisions on a temporary situation. There are many in corporate that I've coached, managed and worked with who thought as they were going through a tough situation that it was going to be permanent and they've made major decisions such as departing prematurely. Shortly after leaving the person who replaced them is considered a hero because of the great results. In many cases it was not due to the replacement but more times than not it was due to good timing for them.

Farmers know that there are four general seasons and they

prepare accordingly. Just like ants instinctively prepare for the winter season during the summer months. If you know it's coming, you can prepare and this helps with confidence and security. Versus if we don't think about the things happening from the perspective of seasons changing it can cause more anxiety than necessary. Many in corporate become discouraged and disappointed at work because their expectations were different from their reality. If we all begin to leverage this analogy it can help us more appropriately adjust our expectations.

REDEEMING THE TIME

In an effort to make the best of our dash (the dash between our birthdate and our death) it's important to make the most of time by going for what's in our heart. Based on my experience, most Individual Contributors (ICs) want to make a positive impact at work by using their gifts, talents and experiences. Many are sitting on great ideas that can make a difference. However, they are hesitant to pursue what's in their heart for fear of the unknown. Others feel that they're too young or inexperienced and others might feel they're too old or it's too late to go for their next level.

One of the objectives of this chapter is to encourage you that it's not too early nor is it too late for you to go for what's in you. When I speak to groups on this subject I get feedback with many great excuses of why people don't go for what's in their heart. Most of it has to do with timing. Many feel their time of opportunities has past and they settle or a younger group who wants to wait until their situation is perfect.

I want to share a few examples for your consideration of various people who made the most of their situation by maximizing their time.

It's not too late or too early for you to go for it!

Some of you may have worked in corporate for years and might feel that you've come as far as you can go. Many may have decided that they are okay with their current level and role and do not want to pursue anything else because they think it's too late. I have coached and worked with many who have posted for different positions and interviewed for higher-level roles in the past and not obtained them. This experience can make them hesitant to go for other new opportunities. They may have gotten to the point of resigning themselves to ride out their last several years until they can get some type of package or get contacted by an executive recruiter for something similar somewhere else.

For those of you who fall into this category, I'd like you to consider the following people who decided to go for their next level in spite of their age or past history of things not going well.

- Abraham Lincoln — Became President of the United States after many failures and challenges
- Ronald Reagan — Became President of the United States when he was almost 70
- Colonel Sanders — Started the KFC Franchise at the age of 65
- Ray Kroc — Became an agent to begin to franchise McDonald's at the age of 52

President Abraham Lincoln

- At the age of 23 he was defeated for state legislature
- At the age of 24 he failed in business
- At the age of 26 his sweetheart died
- At the age of 27 he had a nervous breakdown
- At the age of 29 he was defeated for Speaker of the House
- At the age of 34 he was defeated for nomination to Congress
- At 39 he was not re-nominated after making it to Congress
- At 40 he was rejected as land officer
- At 45 he was defeated for Senate
- At 47 he was defeated for Vice President
- At 49 he was defeated a second time for Vice President
- At 51 he was elected President of the United States

President Ronald Reagan

As many of you know former President Ronald Reagan served in the military, was an actor, and got into politics later in his career. Regardless of his successful career in other areas, he still felt he could offer more and served his second term in office into his 70s. This is encouraging to know it's never too late as long as you're living. It's a matter of leveraging your age and experiences to your advantage. President Reagan is quoted saying to his opponent Walter Mondale during a Presidential Debate, *"I will not make age an issue of this campaign. I am not going to exploit for political purposes my opponent's youth and inexperience."* This is an example of what's possible for all of us.

Colonel Sanders

When Colonel Harland Sanders was 40 years old he was cooking for travelers out of his service station. His cooking fame spread and soon there were huge lines for his food. Sanders then moved across the street to a motel/restaurant to service the high demand. During this time, Sanders had also been tinkering with his special herbs and spices to make the perfect fried chicken.

Fast forward to 1950. The Colonel is 60 years old and has to shut down his restaurant because a new highway was being built where his restaurant was located. Colonel Sanders decided to retire and lived off of social security checks. Not wanting to accept this as his fate, he decided to franchise his chicken at the age of 65.

He started traveling by car to different restaurants and cooked his fried chicken on the spot for restaurant owners. If the owner liked the chicken, they would enter into a handshake agreement to sell the Colonel's chicken. The restaurant would receive packets of Colonel's secret herbs and spices in order to avoid them knowing the recipe. By age 74, Colonel Sanders had 600 franchises selling his trademark chicken. At this time, he sold his company but remained as a spokesperson. At the age of 86, the Colonel was ranked as the world's second most recognizable celebrity. Today KFC is one of the largest food franchises in the world. The Colonel's age did not hold him back.

Ray Kroc

At the age of 52, Ray Kroc began a new age in franchising when he became the national agent for McDonald's. Kroc, making his rounds as a milk shake mixer salesman, came across the McDonald brothers' (Richard and Maurice) small hamburger shop in Southern California. The establishment was simple, serving only a few items: hamburgers, French fries, soft drinks, and milk shakes. These two brothers became one of Kroc's best customers as they purchased several of his machines in his otherwise dying business.

Kroc, curious about why the McDonalds were purchasing so many mixers, investigated the establishment further. Kroc suggested that the brothers expand their presence. As they asked how they could do so, he offered his services as their agent. That is how the little restaurants with the bright yellow arches began. The first shop opened when Ray Kroc was 53 in Chicago, as the organization became the McDonald's Corporation. Six years later Ray bought out the founding brothers.

By the time Ray was 63 there were more than 700 sites in existence across the United States. It wasn't long before McDonald's also caught on in several other countries. By 2003, the corporation held over 31,000 sites in 119 countries. Forty seven million people were being served every day and sales were at a hefty $17 billion.

YOUNG PEOPLE WHO WENT FOR IT

- Steve Jobs founded Apple at age 21
- Mark Zuckerberg set up Facebook at age 20
- President Barack Obama was 47 when he become President of the United States

Steve Jobs

In 1975, 20-year-old Steve Jobs and Steve Wozniak set up shop in Jobs' parents' garage, dubbed the venture "Apple" and began working on the prototype of the Apple I. To generate the $1,350 in capital they used to start Apple, Steve Jobs sold his Volkswagen microbus and Steve Wozniak sold his Hewlett-Packard calculator. Although the Apple I sold mainly to hobbyists, it generated enough cash to enable Jobs and Wozniak to improve and refine their design.

In 1977, they introduced the Apple II—the first personal computer with color graphics and a keyboard. Designed for beginners, the user-friendly Apple II was a tremendous success and ushered in the era of the personal computer.

First-year sales topped $3 million.
Two years later, sales ballooned to $200 million.

At the age of 31, Steve acquired Pixar Animation Studios from George Lucas. After cutting a three-picture deal with Disney, Jobs set out to create the first ever computer-animated feature film. Four years in the making, "Toy Story" was a certified smash hit when it was released in November 1995 when Steve was just 40 years old. Fueled by this success, Jobs took Pixar public in 1996, and by the end of the first day of trading his 80% share of the company was worth $1 billion. After nearly 10 years of struggling, Jobs had finally hit it big. But the best was yet to come and we know the rest of the story.

Mark Zuckerberg

Mark Zuckerberg is one of the five founders of the biggest social networking sites—Facebook. In middle school he began to write software and use computers. He learned basic Atari programming and a tutor had considered him a "prodigy." In high school Mark excelled in his classes and won prizes in astronomy, physics, and mathematics. While he was still in high school, he took a college graduate program in computer programming. He built a program called Zucknet where the computer at home could communicate with his father's computer at his dental practice. He also used his creativity to build computer games often out of ideas his friends would draw for him.

While attending college, he claimed to be able to read and write in Latin, French, Hebrew, English and Greek. His overall knowledge and intelligence helped him excel at college, where he would often recite poems such as the epic "The Iliad." There he was already known as a "programming prodigy" due to the work he had done in high school. He wrote a program he called *CourseMatch* that helped students make decisions about the courses they wanted to take based upon the choices of others and a new website which he called "Facemash." He had several students help him with Facemash including Eduardo Saverin, Andrew McCollum, and Dustin Moskovitz. The site was initially just a Harvard site but soon expanded to other colleges and universities. By 2005 Facemash was known just as Facebook. The site opened up to anyone over age 13 in 2006. By 2007 the site had over 100,000 businesses listing their companies on Facebook and creating pages.

By 2011 it became the largest digital photograph host and had over 350 million accessing the site over mobile phones. On May 18, 2012, Facebook made its IPO (initial public offering). Mark Zuckerberg was named to the 100 wealthiest and most influential people in the world list put out by *Time* magazine in 2010.

President Barack Obama

President Barack Obama became the 44th President of the United States at the age of 47. He was the fifth youngest President of all the U.S. Presidents. Other younger Presidents include Theodore Roosevelt (42), John F. Kennedy (43), Bill Clinton (46), and Ulysses Grant (46). He worked his way through school— Occidental College in Los Angeles, Columbia University in New York, and later, Harvard Law School—with the help of scholarship money and student loans. At the age of 24, Barack Obama moved to Chicago, where he got his start in working in the community. He organized on the city's South Side, working to help rebuild communities devastated by the closure of local steel plants. The President called that time in his life "the best education I ever had, better than anything I got at Harvard Law School." He has credited that experience as crucial to finding his identity—something that shaped his path to the White House.

Barack Obama was elected to the Illinois State Senate at the age of 35. During his time in Springfield, he passed the first major ethics reform in 25 years, cut taxes for working families, and expanded health care for children and their parents. Elected to the U.S. Senate by the age of 43, he reached across the aisle to pass the farthest-reaching lobbying reform in a generation, locked up the world's most dangerous weapons, and brought transparency to government by tracking federal spending on-line. President Obama won a second term as President at the age of 51.

> "Age is an issue of mind over matter. If you don't mind, it doesn't matter." –MARK TWAIN

As these examples demonstrate, regardless of where you are in your career there is an opportunity to pursue your dreams. The examples I listed show that determination, faith and a positive mindset regardless of your season in life can lead to great results. Take time to search out more details about these great people as I've only provided a highlight to inspire the fire within you to not allow your age to prevent you from anything that's a worthy endeavor.

USE ECONOMICS TO JUST SAY "NO"

There are a lot of time management strategies and recommendations. I've read many books on the subject, attended time management classes and seminars as well as purchased the latest technology or app to help me save time. All of these things are great and I think it's worth your time to research it to find what's best for you. Three books that I recommend checking out on the subject are: *Eat that Frog* by Brian Tracy that uses the frog analogy to help us understand the importance of tackling our top priority item first. Determining the biggest, most impactful task of the day and doing it first. The second book is *Time Management from the Inside Out* by Julie Morgenstern. She provides great tips on maximizing your time. The third book is *The 12 Week Year—Get More Done in 12 Weeks than Others Do in 12 Months* by Brian P. Moran and Michael Lennington. This is more of a process to learn about more effective execution but I place it in this time management category because it helps you to maximize your time.

Again, all of these and many others are great and I highly recommend them. However, the one area that I would like to share based on my experience coaching and managing others is the power of saying, no. This is indeed a time management gem. Learning to identify and focus on our top priorities by using our values as the basis for making effective decisions to know what to say yes to and what to say no to help us maximize our limited time. We all only get 24 hours a day and will not get any more.

We have to know that our individual time is ticking!

Every time we say yes to adding something else to our to do list we are potentially diminishing our effectiveness with the other items we agreed to do. When I was getting my MBA, I recall taking an economics class and going into detail on the law of diminishing returns. This is stated as a law or principle, that when any factor of production, as labor, is increased while other factors, as capital and land, are held constant in amount, the output per unit of the variable factor will eventually diminish. Another definition in the dictionary states, any rate of profit, production, benefits that go beyond a certain point fails to increase proportionately with added investment, effort, or skill. This principle confirms the more we add to do, the less effective we become.

I recognize most of us multitask and I'm a work in progress on this one. I also used to think I could do it all such as read email while on a conference call and respond to text messages and online instant messages. All this and I felt I was able to comprehend everything going on. Until one day I was doing all this and a question came up on the conference call directed towards me. I had no idea, and then I realized I was responding to a different person than I intended to in a text and my instant message conversation did not make any sense to the receiver. I eventually got to a point of admitting I had to stop multitasking because I was not giving my best to any of those areas which impacted my personal image with others at work. There are now many studies on the subject of multitasking that highlights how ineffective it can be in work despite that most try to make it work in an effort to save time.

Another economic phrase I'd like to highlight for your consideration in better managing our time is a Cost-Benefit Analysis (CBA). Jules Dupuit, a French engineer, first introduced the concept in the 1930s. It became popular in the 1950s as a simple way of weighing up project costs and benefits, to determine whether to go ahead with a project or initiative. Cost-benefit analysis involves adding up the benefits of a course of action, and then comparing these with the costs associated with it. The results of the analysis are often expressed as the time it takes for benefits to repay costs.

The way the CBA works is assigning a financial value to all of the associated costs and benefits. I like to write in the form of a T-chart. On the left side of the T, I put the costs and on the right side, the benefits. The difference of a CBA and a pro/con list is this is focused on adding a monetary value to the costs and benefits so a business decision can be more effectively made. Adding dollars helps to add another perspective than the traditional pro/con list. My purpose for sharing these ideas is not for us to become economists or try to use these resources to their fullest extent. I'm suggesting the use of these tools as another way to help us make more effective decisions in the utilization of our precious time.

I understand working in corporate, volunteering, serving on boards, participating in extracurricular activities and everything else can make it tough when there's new opportunities. Bearing in mind the law of diminishing returns and conducting a cost-benefit analysis will better equip us to make more effective decisions in an effort to maximize our limited time.

"It ain't over 'til it's over" —YOGI BERRA

THE FAT LADY HAS NOT SUNG!

This is a popular idiom that many people say to essentially reference that it's not too late to win. Things might appear bleak at the moment, but it's not over yet. Based on some online research about this phrase, I learned this relates to the opera's "it ain't over until the fat lady sings."

However, according to an article in the *Washington Post* on June 3, 1978, San Antonio sports writer/broadcaster Dan Cook first came up with the phrase. Dan Cook said it on television in 1978 when the San Antonio Spurs were behind in a series with the Washington Bullets. The Washington Bullets' manager, Dick Motta, repeated it and was widely quoted by the media. By the time the Bullets came from behind to win the finals that year, the saying was on thousands of T-shirts, "fat ladies" were coming to games to cheer the team on, and the proverb's popularity was firmly cemented.

I'm relating this phrase to all of you reading this book. Please understand that the fat lady has not sung as it relates to your career. Regardless if you feel you're too young, inexperienced, too old and over experienced or somewhere in the middle, it's not too late. It's been said that age is a mindset. You can be 70 with a mindset and attitude of a person half your age. For many younger people who dare to go for big opportunities are sometimes referred to as having an "old soul" because of their wisdom at such a young age.

You have the opportunity to choose your course of life and to go for it regardless of your past. Leverage reading this book as your moment of opportunity to choose to have the courage to go for what's in your heart. The future is coming whether we prepare for it or not. Why not prepare to win today by maximizing your time to become all you can be, do and have.

CHAPTER 3

Acres of Diamonds

"Your outlook shapes your life more than your life shapes your outlook." —April Osteen-Simons

Acres of Diamonds is a book written by Russell H. Conwell who founded Temple University. The book is filled with a variety of stories and I will highlight one of the main ideas. In the book it describes a person who was content with what he had in possessions until someone shared what would be possible if he discovered diamonds. This person was eager to find diamonds so he could become rich, as he understood what the diamonds would do for him. As a result, he sold his farm in an effort to go search for diamonds elsewhere.

The person that purchased his property noticed something sparkling in the shallow stream of the brook in the garden. He pulled out a black stone having an eye of light reflecting all the hues of the rainbow. He later discovered that it was indeed a diamond. As he told others, they discovered on the land was a diamond mine. An area full of beautiful diamonds all on the property that was sold by the owner who went to look for diamonds elsewhere.

The original owner who sold the property went off into distant lands and did not find diamonds. Instead he lost all his money, became depressed and ended up taking his life.

Had the original owner of the farm taken the time to better understand what diamonds looked like in their rough form he would have realized he already had what he went out to find. He literally owned acres of diamonds but sold it well undervalue because he did not fully understand what he already possessed. If only he would have better prepared himself by studying diamonds and exploring his property he would have understood that he was already wealthy.

SQUEEZING THE SPONGE

One of the morals of the story is we all have our own acres of diamonds. However, just as the original owner of the property, many of us may have jobs or work in organizations and hear of better opportunities elsewhere and leave in pursuit of what's already available to us where we are currently. Instead of exploring all opportunities and making the best of our current role or company we miss out by departing too soon. Instead we need to choose to exercise patience and have a mindset that all our experiences are part of a path leading us to greatness. It's hard to discover it if we do not take the time to squeeze out everything we can get out of each opportunity. Like squeezing water out of a sponge. When you think you have it all figured out, you may turn it in a different direction or switch hand positions and then you find there was more to get out of it. We should take time to look at our current situation from every viewpoint and do our part to squeeze it out which takes time and effort.

How many of you reading this book can relate? Have you had a decent job or role and were not content or satisfied for whatever reason? Have you left a role like that because someone told you of a better opportunity at another company or functional area? After a short period of time working in the new place you felt as if you were better off where you were. Or, the person who replaced you in your previous position did some great and innovative things and was promoted, recognized, given a raise or whatever it was that you desired. Or, have you left a role after getting a new leader and the new leader ends up in your new organization? Early in my sales career, I was given what was considered tough territories where previous sales reps stated there were not any good opportunities. However, I was happy to have the sales job and uncovered all types of new opportunities and excelled in the same territory where the previous representative underperformed.

All of these are examples of what can happen when we leave a role before ensuring that we are giving it our best and maximizing our potential. I'm not suggesting that we have to stay in our roles indefinitely but stating that we should make the best of our current situation while we are in it. Based on my experience of working in corporate America for over 25 years, I've seen all of these examples and I personally have experienced a few.

LIFE LESSON THAT MAKES YOU SAY, "HMMM ..."

As I was about to graduate from Howard University, I was very blessed to have five different job offers with great Fortune 500 companies including Duracell, J&J (consumer products division), Pitney Bowes, Bristol-Myers Squibb and the Fasson Roll Division of Avery Dennison. I decided to accept a position with Avery Dennison in Painesville, Ohio.

Once I joined, they took great care of me professionally and set me up for success. They had an excellent sales training program; paid for me to get professional voice training and they had me meet with an industrial psychologist to help assess my strengths and weaknesses for development areas. They also placed me in corporate housing during my initial start and provided me with a company car and cell phone. In addition they assigned me to a peer buddy who had been with the company for about 2 years prior to me joining. This person became my mentor and he had recently won recognition as sales representative of the year.

After working in their HQ for almost a year, they assigned me my own sales territory in Cincinnati, Ohio. They set me up to work in a small office with two other experienced sales reps in the area. They both became my mentors to help me get up to speed. It worked out really well. We would go to the office in the morning, then have meetings during the day and return late afternoon to debrief together. We all got along great and supported each other. I was doing well, learning and making or exceeding my sales goal every year.

After working in the field for about 3 years, I obtained a new sales manager who was young, ambitious but in my opinion, not experienced in leading diverse teams of people. In any case, I was not fond of working for him or with him so I began to think about my next move. I was later contacted by an executive recruiter and because I didn't have a strong relationship with my boss, began to see all the negative things about my job and the company. So, when a recruiter contacted me, I was open for discussion. After working for the Fasson Roll Division for 4 years, I decided to leave as I accepted another sales rep position with one of their suppliers based on the executive recruiter selling me on the job.

Many years later, I learned that my first buddy at the Fasson Roll Division was an Executive VP running all of South America for Avery Dennison Corporation. I also learned that another person I knew and worked with who led marketing when I was there became the CEO of Avery Dennison, the parent company of the Fasson Roll Division. When I read about two of the people I knew, it made me think what would have happened had I stayed and made the best of my situation. I know we can't change the past and I'm glad I'm where I am today. However, it's one of those life lessons that make you say, *hmmm* ...

How many of you can relate? Have you been put in situations where at first everything was great, and then with an organizational change or new leadership, everything changed as well as your attitude? How many of you have jumped ship often in pursuit of greener pastures? Whenever situations change we can always remember that we will be the common denominator.

"The primary cause of unhappiness is never the situation but your thoughts about it." —ECKHART TOLLE, *A New Earth: Awakening to Your Life's Purpose*

LEVERAGING YOUR CURRENT ROLE

Again, I get that sometimes we should leave or transition roles and responsibilities. However, I'd like us to first, make sure that we are fully leveraging our current role, seeing the good in it and being grateful for it and giving our best in our current role.

Answer the following questions related to leveraging your current role:

1. Who do you think you work for?
2. What's your purpose for working (in this role specifically)?
3. Which of your strengths are you using at work?
4. What are you doing to develop yourself in your current role and how are you measuring your progress?
5. What do you like most about your job?
6. What are you doing to improve your influence with your peers in this role?

7. What transferable skills are you gaining?

8. What can you do to make this role on your resume appear to be your best of all your positions on your resume?

9. How can you better position yourself in your current role for more recognition?

10. What are you doing to help prepare others to replace you in your current role?

The idea behind these questions is to encourage you to think about your purpose for working in your current role and to spark ideas for making the best of your current position. The question around who do you think you work for is to help us think about our bigger purpose. In coaching sessions, many may initially respond to that first question with their boss' name. Then when I ask who do you really work for they may respond with themselves, their spouse, children, mortgage company, etc. It's helpful to recall the overall purpose for us taking our current position. In most cases there is a bigger plan, purpose or vision. It's a means to an end. Refreshing on it can make a difference in our attitude about our current role depending on how things are currently going and our expectations of our future potential.

The third question on our strengths is for us to recall that work allows us an opportunity of discovering and developing our strong suits. I read and recommend the *Strength Finder 2.0* book by Marcus Buckingham and the Gallup Organization. The book suggests that we lead with our strong suits and not to necessarily focus on our weaknesses. I agree with the concept and have discovered we are more fulfilled when levering our strengths at work. I've learned the importance of bringing all of us to work. Sometimes we have strengths in certain areas that people at work would never know because we leave that part at home. You can always find areas in your current role to leverage or at least use your strengths. Even if you think it's unrelated to the job at hand.

An example is someone with a gift to sing but working in a technical position at work. Having the ability to sing suggests that the person is musically inclined and can figure out ways to incorporate her gift of singing in a technical environment. Maybe during team calls or meetings they can use it as an icebreaker or a pick me up depending on the genre of song. Or, they can use their ability to use their voice in business presentations. They could help other employees use their voice more effectively in communicating verbal messages. They can help others with breathing and speaking from the diaphragm, etc. The thought is to think through creative ways to leverage your natural gifts, talents and strengths.

In leading a team at American Express I learned to incorporate my motivational speaking skills with my direct reports. It happened unintentionally during one of our team calls when I wanted to encourage others who were having a challenging time with their clients. They provided me with feedback that they liked it and would appreciate if I would continue to bring that to our team calls. We made it a normal part of our agenda. I enjoyed it, they enjoyed it and we all benefited. It added another element to help me to leverage my strength and better enjoy my role.

Personal development in our jobs is a difference maker in facilitating getting us from where we are to over the top performance. If you feel that you're already performing at your best, think through what's next or what else can be done to position yourself to be able to replace your boss. There's always something we can do to better prepare ourselves. What classes can you take? What industry conferences can you attend that will stretch you? What type of leadership practices can you institute? Who are you mentoring and whom else can you support? Do you stay up on all the supply chain flow for your industry? How's your competitive knowledge? What else can you do to become a subject matter expert in your industry and job? Personal development focus can help you take the time to think through and access your status to determine what additional things you can do to be more exceptional.

Taking time to think about what you like about your job can go a long way in you appreciating it. Enjoying your job can be motivation to excel in it. In many organizations in which I have the opportunity of coaching others, I meet many who get to a point where they feel their job is just a means to an end. It's what they have to go through to get paid. There was a time in the good ol' days when they enjoyed their work but now it's just a job. In order to help people get refreshed they have to take a fresh perspective of their role. It can happen to anyone but it's important that we watch for the signs so we can adjust and not become a frustrated, unhappy employee.

A few of the leading indicators that you're not happy in your career or losing excitement about your job are the following:

- Gradually showing up late for work, meetings and calls
- Leaving early
- Not participating in team calls and meetings
- Less interactive with team members
- Unwilling to do things together with co-workers outside of the office
- Able to connect with disgruntled employees
- Mediocre performance
- Pushing back often
- Complaining
- Talking about Senior Leaders
- Poor attitude

I recall when I came to a place in my career that I wasn't as happy in my role as I originally felt when I first began. After I was working for American Express for 6 years I had a variety of positions that kept things exciting. I started as an account manager, I was promoted to a national sales director, and then I transitioned to a director of new business development. During that six-year period I reported to 4 different leaders so I experienced a lot of change. In the beginning of each role, I loved it and felt fortunate to have great relationships with my VPs.

Things began to change for me as I was reading non-fiction books, writing in my journal, attending conferences, participating in Toastmasters International, working with an executive coach personally. My interests started changing towards wanting to do something independently. I decided I wanted to become a corporate trainer and this was a little after 9-11 and Amex had outsourced their internal trainers at that time. I started thinking about a new career doing corporate training instead of sales and business development work. I recall, losing interest in the products we were selling and starting to feel as if I was just going through the motions but not really in it.

As my interests started waning so did my effort and desire to over perform in my current role. One day, I remember, my VP scheduled a meeting with me to what he described as us having a "hard" conversation. He asked me if I still wanted to be in my role. He caught me off guard at the time so I gave the corporate response. However, my attitude and work began to reflect how I was feeling internally. There was a time where I had an opportunity to present an overview to the president of our division. I put something together and sent it to my VP for him to review over the weekend. After he read it, he called me and said we need to talk. He went over my presentation with me to show me all the errors he noticed as well as how it appeared aesthetically. I was surprised after I looked it over with him that I actually sent it out in that manner. It was not my best work and he knew I was checking out.

That experience was a wake up call for me. I decided I would stop lying to myself and make a decision on what I wanted to do. I decided to share with my boss and he encouraged me to go for what I desired but to leverage my current role. He helped me to see the opportunities I had to make the best of my current role in preparation for my next whether inside or outside of Amex. He helped me to see the value of having the type of position I had with an opportunity to present to the president of my division. I also had a role that allowed me an opportunity to work with some of the largest companies in world at that time. I was in a role that allowed me to travel throughout the country and to leverage my experiences, gifts and talents in my current job.

As a result, I did set out to become a corporate trainer. However, in the interim I re-engaged in my current role and started performing at my best. As a result, I did get a position with another organization as a corporate trainer but I left Amex on a very positive note. The interesting part is I did return to Amex 6 years later with the endorsement of my last VP. If I didn't change my attitude that door would have been shut. As they say, don't burn your bridges because you may not know what will happen down the road. The other great thing about this experience was when I launched my own business; Amex was one of my first corporate clients. This outcome was a result of making the best of my current situation that ultimately led to what I really wanted.

What hard conversations have you had with your leader or subordinate or that you need to schedule? It starts with looking in the mirror to conduct a self-analysis to determine where you are related to your current role. Then, be honest with your self to determine what makes the most sense for you regarding your career.

Determining what you like most about your job can make a difference in having a better perspective. Part of the process is remembering some of your most enjoyable times at work and the aspects that you like most. In many cases we thoroughly enjoy the main parts of our job and love the organization that has employed us. However, over a period of time with the pressures to meet deadlines, new corporate mandates, higher goals and expectations may put us in a position where we feel overwhelmed and stressed that our focus begins to change to what we enjoy to what we disdain about the role.

It's helpful to recognize that most organizations are now very dynamic with asking everyone to do more with less and to get it done faster and doing it right the first time. All those expectations sometimes place employees in a frenzy and we may not be as excited or motivated to do our best. It can make a difference to recall that it may be seasonal but if it's the new norm we will have to be willing to adjust our attitude about it and learn how best to enjoy this roller coaster ride.

Viewing the ups and downs of the work environment as a roller coaster ride can help. I personally enjoy them because of the anticipation of what's to come around the corner. Knowing we are going to have moments of speeding up, down, around and to each side but this is what makes it exciting. We should have a paradigm shift about it and think about it as a process but being willing to do our part to step up our efforts to meet the challenge.

Many people that I've coached and managed take on the challenge of stepping up their game to meet the new expectations. Others choose not to step up their game and they over a period of time tend to be the ones most unhappy and unfulfilled. Recognize where you are in the process and be willing to adjust as necessary. It's more interesting when we choose to get off the sidelines of complaining and to step into the game. There are many people who have resigned mentally from their jobs but show up to work everyday. We can call them the working dead. They are physically at work but mentally checked out.

There's an old saying of if you can't take the heat then get out the kitchen. In some cases many can't take the heat and instead of getting out the kitchen they choose not to do anything and those are the ones who tend to get in the way of progress and others who make a conscious decision to go for it. I want to encourage you to go for it. The benefits will be worth the effort. It will cause you to pursue personal development and will allow you the opportunity to become a better person.

As we know in going to professional sports games, there are so many of us in the stands that talk trash to the opposing team while at the same time knowing we can't do what they do. We want to distract them with our taunts and booing. We normally don't say anything when they hit their target unless we are hollering at the refs for not calling something that only we saw. I think it's similar to those in the corporate environment who decide not to step up their game, nor to leave to find a better fit. They stay and become naysayers of those making things happen. They're talking about everyone else versus coming up with solutions or solving problems. Let's be sure to not be on that team. Let's choose to be on the winning team by doing our part of making a resolve and taking immediate action as appropriate.

The following are a few questions to ponder and answer regarding your job:

- Think over your career and recall the jobs, companies and situations when you enjoyed your job.
- What was it that you liked in each of those situations?
- What would need to take place for you to be able to enjoy your current role like that again?
- What can you do to help create that environment
- Take away the areas of your job you don't care for and what's the core part of your job that remains? (i.e., being a sales rep and not like the reporting but loving being with clients)
- What can you do to focus more on the aspects you like and getting help on the parts you least enjoy?
- Who do you know that enjoys the functions of the job you don't? What can you do to support each other?

Other considerations for helping to gain a more positive perspective of your current role are to explore leadership opportunities. What can you do to enhance your ability of influence?

One of the definitions of a leader is a person of influence. Influence is being able to leverage your experience or expertise to help others. It's doing things in a manner that provides you with credibility for others to look up to you as an expert or as a go-to person in specific areas. An example would be experienced employees helping to mentor newer employees get up to speed in specific areas. However, it's doing it naturally outside of any specific programs or initiatives. It's having others want to call you for questions based on what they see in you. It's demonstrating expertise and a willingness to share it with others.

All jobs provide experience and aspects of the role that can be leveraged in other positions and in other industries. Understanding the transferable skills that you have and are gaining can provide additional ideas for appreciating your current role. As an example, in a sales role you are developing IQ skills in working with others. This is a transferable skill that can be leveraged in any other position dealing with people or clients. You may use a sales background in a marketing role and many others based on learning skills to persuade others. The transferable skill of persuasion can be used in leadership roles and roles that require negotiation. The more we think through the transferable skills that our role provides the more we can focus on developing and leveraging it for other opportunities that we desire to explore. It helps to appreciate and recognize the skills we are gaining in our current position. It's another way of finding value in our current role to exploit for our future endeavors.

When I decided to pursue a career in corporate training, I was able to leverage my sales background and my Toastmasters experience during the interview to present a business case of how my background fit the desired position. I also tailored my resume for the job working for a corporate training organization. I thought through every type of training I led and participated in as an account manager and sales director. My traditional resume would have highlighted all of my experience and accomplishments as a sales rep, account manager, sales director, and director of new business development. I tweaked it when I wanted to post for an outside position as a corporate trainer. The transferable skills I identified for a training position was my ability to present sales skills that I learned in training classes I attended.

I also was preparing myself in my previous roles in sales. I would volunteer to train on product knowledge or whatever I became strong in and leveraged that experience to position it as I trained others as a sales rep. I created a new version of my resume based on any training I led. I suggest that others do the same as appropriate. Think through your transferable skills related to what you're going for and I'm certain you can identify transferable skills and magnify it on your resume to help you get what you desire.

As you are in your current role and if you have passions for a different type of career, think about how best to use your current role to get the experience that will best position you and your resume. You may have to get creative in thinking through ways to leverage your current position to help you gain experience that will lead to what you ultimately desire. It may be through volunteering, participating on cross-functional teams, creating new projects or initiatives that can aid in your current role be completed more efficiently and effectively.

Look for problems to solve in your current role and business. Explore all aspects of the new career direction and think through parts of it that could meet a need in your current business. Be the one to demonstrate the value it can bring and conduct an ROI on its impact to the business. There may be a win/win for you and your organization by leveraging your transferable skills. That will better position you for your new pursuit. It allows you to gain experience in your current role prior to jumping out the nest.

I recall when I worked in sales roles and I had a desire to become an executive coach and a leadership development corporate trainer, I would explore coaching and training opportunities in my current role. It amazed me as I began to look for it how it seemed to appear before my eyes. As if it was revealed like some thing being unmasked. I would ask for opportunities to attend training sessions. I volunteered to provide high-level updates or to train the trainer for the rest of our team.

Whenever leadership would ask for a volunteer to speak before others or train others, I'd raise my hand. In some cases I'd do my homework and come up with ideas based on books I read that would be a value to the rest of the organization. My leaders really appreciated it and I loved it as I was preparing myself to fulfill my long-term plans.

I want to encourage you to explore opportunities that may

be available to prepare yourself and benefit your current organization. Looking for problems to solve is a great way to begin. Keep your antenna up and you will begin to see what was right before you.

Gaining additional recognition in your current role is typically a result of doing something over and above the norm. Many organizations have all types of recognition programs on various levels. Some provide employees with company points, gift cards, cash awards and various rewards. Some companies offer award trips and other types of incentives to recognize top performers.

Some employees thrive on this and make it a goal to obtain a certain amount of points or to meet the requirements of the award trip. Others don't get into it and find a reason not to want to take advantage of these additional employee attractions.

Beyond the rewards, getting recognized can put you on the radar of senior leaders for promotional opportunities. Many of the recognition or trips include senior level leaders. This normally provides top ranked employees with an opportunity to gain additional exposure to senior level leaders that can open the door for other opportunities.

Based on all of the benefits, what unique, innovative, out-of-the-box types of things can you do to gain more recognition for your efforts? Since you're working anyway, why not take full advantage of stretching yourself and leveraging your full potential in the role for the recognition. I know many people in the middle levels of the workforce might say they would rather be low key and just do a good job without all the fanfare. I dare you to step up your game and be willing to get in this game as I've previously stated. Getting in the game and doing your best allows you to have more fun making the best of your current role which will ultimately open more doors.

Some may feel they are doing great in their job and getting plenty of recognition. My challenge to you is what else can you do beyond what you've already accomplished. Remembering that there is always more we can do if we take out time to think or ask a higher-level leader. Doing more expands your capacity like a rubber band. Expanding our capacity allows us to grow our potential that can lead to expanded responsibilities which leads to more income. Part of obtaining more opportunities is related to outgrowing your job organically. As you are demonstrating leadership you can be helping others along the way that will view you like a boss even while you are their peer. This is succession planning at its best when it naturally happens from doing more and creating additional opportunities for others based on your innovation, accomplishments and gaining new assignments where you are bringing others in to support. This is doing your part to replace yourself in your current role as you are taking on more strategic assignments.

Please know that you can be doing the same job as one of your peers and they can be making over $20,000 more than you annually. It can be significantly more depending on your role, compensation plan and bonus programs. It would be a shame to know someone doing the exact same role as you with the same experience level can be paid much more than you. It's typically based on their recognized contribution level. Those in the game giving it all are typically generating more money. If they're not, you can be assured they will be soon.

Most organizations have a pay for performance compensation structure. It's not about tenure or experience level anymore. It's more about impact to the bottom line and your ability to drive results through others or innovation or some combination.

This is one of the main reasons that I want to encourage you to choose to do your best and provide extra ordinary service. Taking time to ask yourself, "What else?" Working on personal development, sharpening your skills and focusing on continual improvement can and will pay dividends.

It's not necessarily about working hard. It's more about giving your best. When we give our best it might seem to others as working hard, but it should be an enjoyable process to know that you're working at your optimum level. When you are intentionally using your experiences, gifts and talents in your work, you're giving what you have to better the organization that improves you personally. Think about a time at work when you felt very productive. Recall a time when you gave your best on a project, initiative or assignment. How did it make you feel at the end of it? For me, I get a strong sense of accomplishment knowing I did my best. It's especially satisfying when it's well received by others to the point of getting additional income for it. It's a similar statement many parents tell their kids to do in school and it's just as important as professionals in corporate America that we take the same advice for our jobs.

There have been times in my career where I've given my best and there have been times where I did not and I got the results from each. When I was a college student, I obtained a part-time job working for IBM in their marketing department. I was responsible for supporting the marketing representatives and their systems engineers. I mostly helped them prepare their customer presentations, researched information and analyzed client surveys and other miscellaneous tasks as requested. It was a great job and what I call a resume building experience. When I first started, I would come in early, ask to do extra work and I took pride in my efforts to contribute to the team. During my second year, as my classes became tougher, my focus was not totally on doing well at work. Mentally, it transitioned from being a great career opportunity to it just being a job to help me pay for school. As a result of that mental shift, it began to show in my work, efforts and how I showed up.

One day, I came in a few minutes late and the administrative assistant let me know the new Branch Manager wanted to meet with me. I recall it was an attractive young African American lady. When I came in her office she did not smile but asked me to take a seat and she let me have it. I recall her stating the importance of me taking this role serious and showing up to do my best. I countered with I'm a full time student, I just left class and had to take a bus and two trains to get to the office in Bethesda, Maryland, from Washington, DC, blah, blah, blah. She responded that I should work in such a way that they would not know that I'm a student unless I tell them. As far as IBM is concerned, I only work for them and should be grateful to have this opportunity. I thought I felt that way but my work demonstrated different. The new leader let me know that she too was in school getting her MBA through an executive program but none of her marketing reps knew it. She comes in earlier to work and maximizes her time because she has evening and weekend classes. She was taking just as many credits as I was and let me know I should not allow school or anything else to be an excuse for lackluster effort or performance. I sure wish I took her advice to heart at that early age. I heard her but at the time I did not agree with her. I felt she was a type A, workaholic and didn't have a life outside of IBM. As I obtained work experience over the years, I learned the hard way to agree with her philosophy. However, I only support it to the extent of giving your best in an effort to maximize your full potential.

I also want to bring out the point about doing your best regardless of your role or the company where you're currently employed. Some may think in my previous example, that if you worked for an IBM type company as a college student you would have understood to make the best of it. However, my road to getting a job at IBM as a college student began when I was a high school student working for McDonald's. McDonald's was my first real job outside of being a paperboy when I was a junior in high school. I loved McDonald's as a kid and always looked forward to working for them. When I got the job as a teen, I did my best. I started out working in the back flipping burgers. I later had an opportunity to work the registers and did extremely well and I was faithful in opening and closing the store. After my first year, I received the employee of the year award. During my second year working for McDonalds I was asked to lead the production and received the most courteous employee award. I leveraged this experience during my interview with IBM that helped to seal the deal of me getting my IBM gig. If I had the attitude working for McDonald's in high school just as many others did, I would not have been able to have it on my resume and use it during my IBM interview.

Doing your best in your current place opens doors to your future space. My college roommate worked for FedEx loading packages and years later became a VP for them. A close friend started working in a supermarket in high school packing bags and years later became a general vice president for this same grocery chain. Take a moment to think through your early work experiences or of others you know that started out small, made the most it, and it helped to open doors for where they are today. Don't despise small beginnings, as they can be your acres of diamonds in disguise.

Your work philosophy goes with you regardless of your position or level. It also has impact in other areas of your life. Generally, if you're not organized at work by having a ton of emails in your inbox not filed into folders, there's a big chance your personal emails are that way. If your emails are unorganized, it stands to say there's a high probability your personal mail that's delivered to your place of residence is probably all over your desk or wherever you store your mail before sorting it. I'll ask for those of you who fit into this category with me to say, amen! If you don't fit into this category, I'm sure you know others who do or you can relate to the point but your example may be in another area. The idea is for us to raise our standard of excellence in our current role so it becomes our way of operating.

Working as a people leader, I recall conducting an annual calibration of people in the same level and role. I rank the top 10% in the top category and the bottom 10% in the bottom category that typically puts them in a bucket of having to go through a performance improvement plan. The far majority of the ranked employees are considered relatively speaking "average." Sure there are variations in the 80% but their rating remains the same. This is generally the group of people who are doing a good job in at least meeting or slightly exceeding their goals and expectations. They're doing more than enough to keep their job and are great team players and contributors. However, in order to get out of that middle box, over the top performance is the bar. Most are in the middle and doing the status quo, which typically means to be willing to give your best over a period of time can better position you for the best ratings which tend to lead to promotional opportunities with consistency.

Another area of consideration for making the best of your current role is being grateful for it. The more we recognize the good in our current role and have an appreciation for it, the more we will want to do our best. Most start out valuing their role but as time goes on, issues come up, new leaders take over, our feelings may begin to wane. It's a natural thing that happens to many so it's important for us to recognize it and to remember to find something good about it to be thankful for having.

One of my experiences that helped me really appreciate having a job was when I actually needed a job and didn't have one. As I've shared, I left corporate to start my own business but as a result of the 2009 recession, I lost most of my clients. Things got really tight financially so I started exploring with my client base and other companies in the Bay area. At first, I was not finding any companies who were hiring for positions in which I had an interest. It created more concern and a strong sense of urgency. I leveraged my connections and eventually obtained another position with American Express as a Sales Director.

At times, I felt desperate and was willing to consider lower level positions, so when I was able to get a position at the same level I left Amex 6 years prior, I was grateful and appreciative. I had a paradigm shift regarding work. In the past I never had a problem getting a job and had not been in many situations where I needed a job. Then I was in a situation during the recession and not as many companies were recruiting. It let me know how fragile things can be and personally learning the impact of not having a job. In addition to not having regular income, not working also had an impact on my sense of contribution in a work environment. I missed the camaraderie of the corporate environment and working with others. It's ironic that's what I missed and sometimes when I was in that environment that was also the part that would get to me. As they say, "It's not until you don't have something that you learn to appreciate it more."

Take time to think about how having a job is helping you positively. Not only from the financial benefits but think of the other benefits. Additional considerations would be an opportunity to contribute and to work with other smart and diverse people, to learn new skills and gain additional experiences. Sometimes after working in a role for an extended period of time, we may forget all the good it's doing for us because our focus is on the opposite. It's important for us to take time to think about what we are grateful for regarding our current job. It will help us to better value it to enhance your motivation for wanting to bring your best to the table.

This exercise needs to take place over the next 7 days. Take time each day to write at least 10 things you're grateful for about your current job for the next 7 days. You may do it anytime during the day or a little throughout the day. The more you are able to capture in writing, the better. It will cause you to recognize what you did not notice previously and it will give you a chance to gain new insights and ideas to thrive again where you are currently. Again, this approach will better position you for bigger and better opportunities because you're discovering your acres of diamonds.

What I am grateful for about my job today:

_____

_____

_____

CHAPTER 4

Let it Go!

"Holding on to anger is like grasping a hot coal with the intent of throwing it at someone else; you are the one who gets burned."
—SUPPOSEDLY BUDDHA

WORKING AS AN EXECUTIVE COACH allowed me the opportunity to work with many mid-level individual contributors and people leaders. Some were considered high potentials and others were thought of as people the firm was considering releasing and others were somewhere in the middle of those two categories. In coaching all types of people in corporate, I learned the majority of the challenges people experience are related to core issues. They typically share with me all the surface related things they're dealing with and it takes effective questioning and time to get to the core. In some cases they recognize their main issues and in other cases they're uncertain what's the cause of them having some of the feelings they do about their job and future prospects.

According to the *Encyclopedia Britannica,* an iceberg is a floating mass of freshwater ice that has broken from the seaward end of either a glacier or an ice shelf. We only see about 10% of an iceberg since 90% of an iceberg is below the surface. It can take 5–10 years for it to form and they can last over 50 years.

Image Credit: Ralph Clevenger

This can be related to what is exposed in a corporate environment. Like an iceberg, we typically share about 10% of ourselves with others. Going deeper is normally from building relationships over a period of time. I like demonstrating this in workshops by asking someone to role-play with me what happens on many Monday mornings at work. I'll approach someone and say, "Hey Justin, how was your weekend?" As soon as Justin begins to respond, I see another co-worker I need to talk to about a project so I immediately turn my attention to catch the other person. Justin is left standing alone shaking his head thinking why did he bother to respond.

I ask people in the workshop if they can relate and most respond that it happens all the time. It gives the impression that it's all about the business at hand. We are courteous, but really only care about getting our jobs done.

This does not build relationships but keeps us at the surface level with others. It creates an environment of business only. Despite our position at work, it's just one dimension of our multifaceted roles in life.

Part of coaching is allowing an opportunity to take time to focus exclusively on those being coached; where they are personally and where they are in business. Most appreciate the opportunity to share what's going on in their personal lives and how it impacts or relates to their work life. Coaching allows opportunity to go beneath the surface to better access the root causes to some of their work related challenges.

There are many great leaders in corporate that are skilled at getting to the core issues in a professional manner—however, based on my experience of coaching others, this is not the norm.

Since most interact at the 10% above the surface level we tend to work through issues with a band-aid approach since we have not taken the time to go deeper. Examples can include a project manager who was previously a top performer but over the last few months has been consistently missing deadlines.

The traditional response may be to place him on a performance improvement plan when in reality the root cause might be related to him going through a recent separation. As a result of the relationship being surface level this has not been shared nor has the question been asked if there is something going on preventing him from meeting his deadlines. The way this can play out if not discussed is the leader puts them on a plan and if they don't meet the requirements they are let go. However, on the other hand if there is a below the surface relationship, this could have been addressed to help the project manager get the needed assistance on the projects and personally. He's a previous top performer that the firm could have lost.

There are a variety of core issues that many people deal with in working in corporate. One of the most common that I've discovered through coaching is forgiveness. It's when people hold on to grudges and hurts from the past and are unwilling to let it go to move on productively.

As I was coaching, I would often hear comments around things their boss did to them that in their eyes were wrong, inappropriate, hurtful, mean or disrespectful. Whenever I coached employees who were being considered for a performance improvement plan, this type of attitude was prevalent. Most would complain about their leaders in some form of mistreatment. I would listen up to a point and then help them to see what they were doing to themselves by holding on to the mistreatment versus taking accountability for their part and being willing to change it by letting go of their hurt and moving forward in a positive way. Many in corporate take on a victim mentality from a past low performance review, being put on a performance improvement plan or some other type of poor rating.

There are a lot of people working in corporate who are hurt by things co-workers did or did not do for them. Some are hurt from getting passed over for promotions, not getting a raise, not being selected to do things or participate on groups or promotions, not getting recognition, lack of support and a variety of other things. Many are legitimate and some may not be merited. Regardless, what may become a core issue for a poor attitude in many cases is based on issues like these that have not been addressed. The poor attitude tends to be a result of unforgiveness. It's holding on to past hurts and waiting for some type of restitution or for the person to come to them and apologize or to acknowledge the error of their ways. However, that may or may not happen and it prevents their ability to let it go.

From my coaching experience, I've concluded that forgiveness is a big core issue in the work environment. According to *Merriam-Webster* dictionary, forgiveness is to cease to feel resentment against an offender; to grant relief; to pardon. I define it as releasing any repayment of wrong and making a decision to let it go.

There are many studies on the impact of unforgiveness and what it does to people. According to the Mayo Clinic the benefits of forgiveness are the following:

- Healthier relationships
- Greater spiritual and psychological well being
- Less anxiety, stress and hostility
- Low blood pressure
- Fewer symptoms of depression
- Stronger immune system
- Improved heart health
- Higher self-esteem

According to the Mayo Clinic some of the effects of unforgiveness are:

- Bring anger and bitterness into every relationship and new experience
- Become so wrapped up in the wrong that you can't enjoy the present
- Become depressed or anxious
- Feel that your life lacks meaning or purpose, or that you're at odds with your spiritual beliefs
- Lose valuable and enriching connectedness with others

Forgiveness is a choice that allows you to get anger, hurt, resentment, depression, frustration, bitterness, grudges, hostility and anything other negative emotion or response out of you. Forgiveness benefits those who choose to forgive regardless if the offender apologizes or acknowledges their error or not. It's a proactive decision that liberates you from the person who inflicted the pain.

The interesting thing I discovered is in most cases the person who caused the offense either doesn't know the pain they caused, doesn't care or has forgotten about it and moved on doing well in their career. Unforgiveness is something that can prevent many from moving forward in their career or even enjoying their job. It can be a paralyzing force if not recognized for what it really is to us. Many may not choose to view it this way and will likely continue to go from job to job, company to company and not be satisfied with their leadership or co-workers. It's likely related to experiencing offense and running away from the core issue rather than acknowledging it and choosing to forgive.

I've had many experiences throughout my career of being offended and having to deal with conflict in the work environment. I shared in a previous chapter how I left my first job outside of college primarily because of a new leader offending me. He would make comments to me on things I considered to be racist statements. I've had other experiences like a VP who would make comments about how long me and others would last in our new roles after starting in a new director level position. I've had previous leaders not speak to me for missing goal one year and a variety of other things that I could have held on to if I wasn't careful. Now don't get me wrong, all these things impacted me and hurt and my initial reaction wasn't always the best. In some cases I did post out and leave until I learned to acknowledge my feelings and make a choice to forgive and let it go. I stopped running away from people like that and learned to remain authentic to my natural upbeat self. Letting it go and remaining in a happy and joyous mood allowed me to outlast the leader who commented about how long I'd last. It allowed me to get promoted away from the leader who would not speak to me after missing my goal one year. It allowed me to thrive in the face of my detractors and to later build better relationships with them.

It also works both ways. You may be the one who could potentially offend another employee. It might not be intentional but in the normal course of business, things happen. When I was promoted at Wells Fargo to lead a team of business bankers, there was a business banker who was a top performer and went for the same position. I was considered an outsider since I had only worked for Wells for about 7 months before being promoted. I did not have any previous banking experience and was promoted to lead a team of business bankers. This employee could have taken on a negative attitude as I later learned this was the second time he posted for this position and did not get it. The previous time he lost it to a peer and this time to an external candidate without experience working as a business banker. I sensed some initial resistance and was concerned that he may have become a disgruntled employee and not want to perform for me.

I responded by acknowledging how I thought he might have felt about me getting the role and his future with the firm. I chose to confront it head on and to have an open discussion with him about it. As a result, I made him a team lead and leveraged his experience to help me as a new leader to the team. I didn't make any promises, but I did agree to do my part if he did his part by continuing to exceed his objectives and to help me get up to speed in which he complied.

Three years later when I decided to leave and run my own business full-time, I was able to get him promoted to replace me and he continued to excel and be promoted over the years. The last time I heard from him, he was promoted and at the SVP level. What if he focused on the fact that in spite of him being a top performer as an individual contributor and that he went for this position twice and did not get it. Staying focused on those facts could have allowed thoughts of frustration, things don't work out, the man is holding him back, this company does not appreciate him, etc. He could have taken his feelings out on me by deciding not to give his best and would have hurt his career in the long run.

Instead, after several heart to heart one on ones with me, he decided to let go of the past and give me a chance to help him develop in areas that might have prevented him from getting to the next level. Without letting go of his hurts he could have stagnated his career. I want to make sure we all understand the potential impact of holding on to things that come up in the workforce.

The sooner we can release the blame and take full accountability for our part, the sooner we can be back on the road to enjoying our jobs and positioning ourselves for a bright, career future.

Holding on to grudges keeps us trapped in thinking small and not being able to see the forest from the trees. I had an opportunity to meet the CEO of American Express, Ken Chenault. When I was an employee working in New York, I was randomly selected with a group of 11 other employees to have lunch with Ken and ask him questions. I recall asking him about how the meetings at his level tend to go. He shared that many outsiders might think they're arguing. Ken let us know they debate and have spirited disagreements and dialogue. However, this is how they discuss a point or an initiative.

When they break from the meeting, they go to lunch, hang out together and all is good. However, the way their meetings go could give a different impression. I became aware that at the highest levels of corporate is a stress-induced environment that can create more opportunities for conflict and offense. They seem to understand at the higher levels that it's okay to disagree in a meeting and to butt heads on various topics. However, no one holds on to it and they learn to move on to the next thing at hand while continuing to work together and collaborate to do what's best for the business.

It's important for us all to keep in mind that as long as we work in corporate that offenses will come. We will have conflict in our work environment and the better we can deal with it the better off will be our careers. I also understand that most get that it's important for us to be able to handle it. However, we all could use tools and information on better dealing with it and learning to let it go. I've heard many people use the phrase, "I'll never forgive them for that." Not realizing that sentiment is doing more harm than good.

Understanding that offenses will happen and mentally preparing for how you will conduct yourself when they do, can definitely be helpful. It reminds me of a position I had at American Express working as a director of business development with large strategic accounts. These were companies with annual revenues over $2B who had many layers, decision makers and influences to finalize a decision. My objective was to sell in financial service solutions to help them with automated solutions to become more efficient. Sometimes it would take up to a year of work to sell in the concept. Once I would get buy-in from the business unit, they would inform their legal group who would create an agreement for us to do business together. In many cases we would have to take another few months to complete the negotiations of the business arrangement. The idea was for us to resolve any disagreements in advance of them happening. We would outline our terms and conditions for working together. We preferred to begin with our template and in some cases they preferred to use their template.

The idea is that most business contracts set out the terms and conditions for doing business together with provisions included to resolve potential differences. In business, disagreements happen and people could take offense but the terms and conditions allow us to have something to refer to in the event we have an issue. It's interesting how when we are in the early phases of establishing a business partnership how most are excited about being able to work together that the business unit or sales person wants to do whatever it takes to make it happen.

Thankfully, we have corporate attorneys whose job is to protect the company with agreements, terms and conditions and arbitration clauses in the event something changes down the road. I did have a situation occur with a large corporation that I was able to establish a relationship. After about a year, they had some major organizational changes and new leadership did not view our agreement as a strategic initiative. We had a 5-year agreement in place and they came asking to get out of the agreement. Prior to contacting me, they reviewed our contract in place to explore what were the parameters around an exit clause. We were able to resolve the situation in an amicable manner because of the pre-negotiations of the contract.

As a company puts things in place to protect their interests in case things change down the road, so should we in cases of issues that arise for us at work. The thought is to come up with some of our own "T&Cs" with the foundation to be based on choosing to forgive – no matter what happens. It's part of the process of dealing with conflict and understanding your natural style for resolving issues. I'm not asking that we simply let go without taking the necessary steps to get resolution or emotional healing. I'm not suggesting if someone does something intentionally that was offensive or hurtful that we do not address it directly. We should look to get resolution and do our part to obtain justice when it's necessary. However, regardless of the outcome it will make a big difference for us to choose to forgive for our sake and not the perpetrator.

> When you forgive, you in no way change the past—
> but you sure do change the future.
> —BERNARD MELTZER

When working as a leadership development coach, I focus on supporting work teams to become more cohesive to work as a unified, high performing team. I normally share topics for me to cover with the decision maker to allow them an opportunity to pick and choose from modules that I've created. The majority of the time they will ask that I cover a session of conflict resolution for their team.

When I interview the decision maker in preparation for the workshop, they typically inform me of some of the various types of conflict that they deal with in their work team. Some of it is related to disagreements during team meetings, issues that a few team members have with each other and differences of opinions between the leader and the team members. Part of the process I do is to have them complete a conflict management assessment to help determine how they normally deal with conflict. What I've learned through this process is we all handle conflict differently based on our background and previous experiences dealing with conflict.

Take time now to think about your experiences dealing with conflict at work and answer the following questions:

1. Describe the situation.
2. When was it and what was going on in your life at that time?
3. Where did it take place?
4. How did it make you feel and why?
5. What did you do about it?
6. How was it resolved and what part did you play?
7. If it's not resolved, why not and what can you do to bring resolution to it now?
8. What have you learned about how you deal with conflict?
9. Looking back on it after reading this chapter, what would you do differently?
10. Capture your take-a-ways in the form of a plan of action for how you will manage conflict going forward.

These questions will provide you with insight about how you internalize and manage conflict. Be honest with your self-assessment and develop thoughts on what you will do differently based on how you're currently wired to handle conflict. Many of us handle conflict head on and as soon as it happens. Others may not immediately respond but take time to analyze then respond. Some may not be comfortable with directly addressing it based on their personality or background. Whatever your natural tendency, it's important that you understand it. This allows you to adjust as needed based on the offense.

I learned that my natural tendency in the past when dealing with conflict was to avoid it. In other words, if someone did something to me that I found offensive, I would simply stop dealing with the person. Rather than confronting and dealing with it directly, I would do my best to avoid the person or the subject. I would keep my distance and would only interact if I had to. I later discovered that avoiding is not solving or addressing anything. It could cause that issue to continue to occur. Based on that knowledge, I began to become proactive in addressing offense by letting the person know I was offended. I would do my best to address it professionally and without causing any additional offense to the other person involved. It began with me first acknowledging my natural tendency. I uncovered it from answering the above questions, from reflecting on my journal entries and from direct feedback from others who have interacted with me.

Your natural tendency is what it is today. It's worth your effort to determine if you are a person who avoids dealing with conflict, if you are inclined to address offense directly, if you are the type who does not want to cause any discomfort to others and you placate to keep them happy or if you do your best to ensure everyone wins through collaboration. Understand what it is and be on the look out for actions that you do that demonstrates it. Based on your analysis be aware of others' natural style in dealing with conflict. Think about how you would assess your boss' conflict management style. What about your co-workers' style, direct reports or others you regularly interact with for work? It tends to be easier to deal with someone who has the same conflict management style as you but more challenging when dealing with someone whose style is different.

Think about working with someone whose conflict management style is to constantly give in to you or anyone else who offends him or her. If you do something intentional that you know will offend this person and their natural style is to accept whatever, not say anything or put the blame on themselves. Your conflict style is to dominate the conversations, you're very vocal, self confident and direct. I'd imagine if you as a dominator dealt with an obliger that it would frustrate you and you would be inclined to walk over them so to speak. Or, if your style is to collaborate, to try to get everyone to work more effectively together and you had someone on your team who is an avoider. I'm sure that would be a challenging situation to resolve as well.

However, it can all be managed effectively as long as we are aware of both our and the other person's conflict resolution style. Taking a moment to assess where the other person is and being sure to address the issue at hand and not consider it the person who can make a difference. In my experience in coaching clients through conflict management, it's important that they put the focus for resolution on the issue and not the person. As an example, if I screw up on one project, this does not make me a screw up. I've seen clients place a label on others based on their experience and try to change the other person. Versus, putting the focus on changing the issue in collaboration with the other person that solves the problem. Otherwise, we are placing bandages on deep vitally inflicted wounds. Getting to the core of an issue is what will solve the problem long term versus not being on the same page in working together to solve the agreed upon issue.

Gaining agreement on exactly what the issue at hand is not as easy as you might think at first glance. I've worked with people who had what they considered to be an issue in working with one person as their lack of responsiveness. The other person felt the issue at hand was that the other person emailed them too much instead of picking up the phone. Once they got together face to face they uncovered what the true issue was for them. In this example it was their preference for communicating with each other. One person was more of a just ping me with any questions and let's keep things moving type. The other was more relationship oriented and preferred direct contact to discuss any questions so they could hash it out together. As you are managing through a conflicting situation ensure you get consensus on the problem at hand so you both can properly address the root cause.

Most understand that unforgiveness is not ideal and it's not like we are looking to hold on to grudges, be bitter or resentful. It naturally happens in the course of interacting with others on any given day and at any given moment. Things happen, intentionally, yes, but I think in most cases unintentionally. In the work environment, it can happen in a variety of ways.

Following are a few examples that you may be able to relate to that created offense for me while working:

• I had to present a business unit review to my general manager with my peers. I did a thorough job of preparing by getting input from all of my direct reports, I stayed up late doing analysis and I was scheduled to be on PTO the day of the event but I sacrificed my personal commitments to attend this very important meeting. The day of the presentation, the general manager shows up 20 minutes late, attends alone and doesn't bring a notebook. After I did my best in sharing the results-that happened to be the best in the region-he simply says, "good job." After my peer presents results that were last in the region, the general manager asks him to plan to present some of his best practices on the GMs next national call. This caused me to feel underappreciated and my work not valued and my time not respected.

• There was a senior level sales position I was going through a thorough interview process for. I met with the hiring manager, with his boss and even got an endorsement from the head of the organization. As a courtesy, the hiring VP asked me to interview with another VP in a different functional area who led a team of account development individuals that I would partner with on client opportunities. I'll call this other VP, John. John was scheduled to fly from Los Angeles to Oakland to meet me. The morning of our interview he had his assistant call me to say he was not going to make it. We scheduled a follow-up interview over the phone and he came across as sarcastic and negative. He shared how he didn't think the new position I was interviewing for would last long. After I shared my goal was to do a great job in this position and then after a few a years to explore leadership roles, he responded it would take a lot longer than my plan. I felt everything I said he would have said the opposite. I got the job and scheduled monthly calls with John who would constantly cancel at the last minute. He was not cooperative or supportive at all. This continued until he was eventually let go from the company. In this situation, I wanted to avoid working with this VP because he made me feel undervalued.

• The third area of offense for me at work was related to getting a low performing sales territory in what I considered to be the boonies. When I first started working in sales I did not realize they sometimes give the new hire the territory no one else wants. I was hired in a professional sales role and spent over 10 months in training in the HQ. Ten months was longer than the typical time frame for new hires to be trained. I expressed an interest in working in a sales territory on the East Coast or the West Coast. After waiting and hoping to be in an area of choice they assigned me to cover essentially most of central and southern Ohio and Kentucky. Areas I did not have any desire to cover. When I started to travel throughout the territory, I uncovered it was covering clients in very remote areas in small towns in which it would take me hours to drive and cover. Initially, I was excited to get the job until I learned about everyone else's territory that was more established and overall, better geographies. I felt that I was treated unfairly and was upset with the company until I learned to make the best of the situation.

These are three different examples of my experiences of being offended at work. During the time I went through each of the scenarios it was a hard time for me. I simply was looking for a job that would offer me a fair opportunity to do my best by working hard and being recognized and rewarded for my efforts. These different incidents happened at different times during my work experience. One was during my first job after graduating, another occurred after I worked for years and the other was during my later years in corporate.

Research states that we spend most of our life at work. According to Gallup.org, the average workweek is 47 hours. Knowing that there is 24 hours a day, 7 days a week. According to the Department of Labor and Statistics, the average amount of sleep we get on a daily basis is 7.7 hours and if we are working 8.7 hours a day, that leaves us with 7.6 hours of time at home with family and friends. This does not include time commuting to work, eating, on social media, etc. The point I want to make is we spend the majority of our time at work. This creates plenty of opportunities for offenses to occur and it happens to everyone. The higher you are in the organization, the higher the probability that you may be the cause of it for others. Generally speaking, the higher levels seem to be able to more effectively deal with conflict and know how to move beyond it without holding grudges. They seem to have a better understanding that it happens but they don't let it stop their progress by holding on to issues.

One of my assignments working as a leadership development consultant for a large client was to attend monthly operating review meetings with the Chief Procurement Officer and all of his VPs. The CPO asked me to evaluate the effectiveness of their meetings and to provide insights and recommendations to help them perform more as a unified high performing team. Afterward, I provided some feedback that included how nice all the VPs were towards each other. They were actually too nice. What I discovered is they had an unspoken rule that when one would give their review, the others would only make positive comments or not say anything at all. No one challenged each other. It was almost to say, if you don't mess with me, I will not mess with you when you present.

After discussing with the CPO, he stated he wanted to instill conflict in the group. He would prefer that they begin to think more broadly about the organization instead of just focusing on their respective areas. He wanted them to care enough about the business to push back on each other even when he's not present. When I first presented the concept of inducing conflict in their monthly ops review meetings they seemed concerned. I later shared some of the positive aspects of conflict and how they can help a business or team.

Some potential positive side effects of instilling conflict in a work team are the following:
- Group culture can become more unified
- Improved group problem solving
- Team engagement is enhanced
- Team contributions increase
- Increased knowledge and experience about the broader

business

- Group culture can become more unified

"Individual commitment to a group effort—that is what makes a team work, a company work, a society work, a civilization work." —VINCE LOMBARDI

The U.S. became more unified as a country going through the events of September 11, 2001. During that time, I worked in Manhattan and my regular commute was a train ride to the World Trade Center where I would walk a few blocks to my office building at American Express. On that day, I was on an Amtrak train headed from New York to Washington, DC, for a client meeting. I was notified of the plane crashing into the tower from a phone call from home and many others on the train received the same call. The train stopped in Baltimore and let everyone off stating they would not be able to go any farther due to the unfortunate events.

I was traveling with a group of colleagues and we went to the car rental counters and learned they were all sold out. A person who lived in the area offered to give us a ride to a rental car location in the suburbs as a way to help. The rental car location provided us with a one-way rental but did not charge extra due to the events of that day. We drove back to the New Jersey area to drop off each other. It was a strange day where everyone was nice and extremely helpful. It was like we were all friends willing to do whatever we could for each other. This catastrophe created a sense of unity as Americans. Once people began to fly regularly again there was a big change in security at airports and most were glad to comply with the new rules. We all understood the purpose and wanted to do whatever we could to cooperate.

This example demonstrates that going through some tough situations with others can cause a group to become more unified. When everyone is working towards the same goal and face unforeseen obstacles and especially when you succeed as a team, it causes a group to be more solidified like a sports team. The success of a team is based on the results of each of the individuals doing their part to contribute. It's a sense of everyone leveraging and sharing his or her strengths for the betterment of the whole team.

IMPROVED GROUP PROBLEM SOLVING

> "Teamwork is the fuel that allows common people to attain uncommon results." –ANDREW CARNEGIE

I provide various types of services with Over the Top Coaching that include executive coaching, communications skills training, conflict resolution, change management, sales training, coaching skills for managers, motivational speaking, conflict management and team building workshops. The most requested of all the services I've provided to Fortune 500 companies over a 5-year period has been team-building workshops. Most companies that I've worked with see a need to help their teams work more cohesively together. I've done assessments in preparation for team building workshops and discovered many of the team members initially consider their work groups to be dysfunctional. Many people in a work group consider it to be the leader's fault. However, based on my experience that's a misconception. Getting everyone to understand the dynamics of a team is based on all the individual team members and not just the team leader. The leader can set the vision and the tone but the members of the team create the culture. The more the group works together through their challenges by focusing on solutions for the team the more cohesive they become.

Some of the exercises I do in team building workshops allow the team members to get to know each other in a much deeper manner. They share their core values, interests outside of work, preferred communication style and we explore opportunities to help them build trust with each other. I recall during one session how the "C" level executive just learned that one of his employees who he worked with for over three years spoke fluent French. He was shocked to find out they both had that in common but they never took the time to get to know each other outside of work. In some cases I get resistance in some of these types of exercises because many have the mindset to leave out the personal in business. However, this is a big mistake as we are all people who have lives outside of the office. Going deeper to learn of each other helps team members better understand how best to work with one another, ultimately fostering improved group problem solving.

TEAM ENGAGEMENT IS ENHANCED

"Talent wins games, but teamwork and intelligence wins championships." –MICHAEL JORDAN

The Gallup organization has an employee value survey that is given at many major corporations. One question that I recall asks, "Do you have a best friend at work?" When I first learned of that question, I didn't understand how that applied to engagement until I researched it. The idea behind that question is related to internal connections with others who have something in common. The more close, internal relationships, the higher likelihood an employee will stay and be more engaged. It provides them with someone to vent with as needed without the fear of retribution.

I use this as an example of how conflict can enhance team engagement. Individuals on work teams who have great personal relationships can create an environment where they're more open to be vulnerable with each other. This fosters more risk taking that can create big wins for the overall group. The opposite of which, when team members are not willing to take risks or be vulnerable can create a working culture of lone rangers focused on their personal success rather than the betterment of the team. Team engagement is enhanced when relationships can be fostered so everyone feels a sense of connection to each of the team members.

Team contributions increase.

"The strength of the team is each individual member. The strength of each member is the team."
—PHIL JACKSON

Phil Jackson was the coach of the Chicago Bulls when Michael Jordan was on the team. Phil was known as one of the best coaches in the NBA and won 6 championships. He transitioned to the LA Lakers where he had a team full of some of the best players in NBA history. However, they initially did not work together as a cohesive or unified team. They had all the talent needed and all the members of the team could each hold their own in their respective positions. Phil Jackson considered this one of the biggest coaching challenges because of the big egos he had to deal with. Phil worked on enhancing team relationship by leveraging everyone's strengths. He had to help them all see and understand the benefits of team cooperation and supporting each other. Once he was able to get everyone in alignment, they were able to win 3 championships in a row.

Dealing with conflict on a work team can be worth the effort. Learning to leverage the strengths of each individual player can allow for each member's contribution to increase. When everyone steps up their game it causes the whole team to step up their results.

INCREASED KNOWLEDGE AND EXPERIENCE ABOUT THE BROADER BUSINESS

"Coming together is a beginning. Keeping together is progress. Working together is success."
—HENRY FORD

Going through conflict as a team can also lead to increased experiences and knowledge. Gaining wins as a team can help improve team dynamics and results. Celebrating team wins as a team increases knowledge and provides momentum to build on for each member. It's like creating memorable experiences for a family by going on vacation. During the time away, each family member will get to spend quality time with each other outside of the normal environment that can facilitate enhanced dialogue and relationships. Viewing the photos from the trip allows an opportunity to reminisce on what happened and some of the challenges that came up. At the time the challenge happened the family members were not happy. However, reflecting on the situation at a later time typically causes a laugh and a more positive perspective from the experience.

As a work team we can learn the same concept. To view our past challenges and accomplishments as learning opportunities, can help everyone see the bigger picture. Taking time as a team to reflect on past accomplishments as a team allows the ability to see things they may not have noticed in the moment. Viewing past challenges and success as a team as well as discussing areas of opportunity helps build for the future of the business. Conflict in a business environment can be good for the business if the team member chooses to leverage the experience and to learn from it for the good of the team moving forward.

Positive conflict is when the group is on one accord with the vision of the organization and committed to its success. It also makes a difference when there is trust among the team members. If everyone understands the goal is to support each other in the attainment of their individual goals, conflict can make a positive difference.

LETTING GO

Releasing any hurt feelings, bitterness, grudges, and resentment allows us to move forward and embrace what lies ahead.

In my career, I've relocated over five times with different companies to major cities across the U.S. When I look up the top stressful life events, moving is always on the top of the list. Moving is stressful because it's a disruption to a typical routine regardless of the reason for the move. Any life change, even for good reasons, induces stress. Based on my experience of moving I normally go through a process of deciding what to get rid of so I don't have to take it to the new location. Initially, I had a habit of holding on to things that I've had for years even if I hadn't used them in a long time. I also had sentimental value to my previous residence with memories of my various experiences living in that location.

I recall when I first moved to California from New Jersey, I missed my larger home on the East coast and the change of seasons. I eventually learned to appreciate having the opportunity of living on the West coast, but began to embrace my current place. When I made a mental transition to make the most of my current location, I began to enjoy it. However, it wasn't until I made a shift in my perspective of letting go of the old to embrace the new. I recall going through this process each time I moved to a new city. There always seemed to be a period of time to make the mental shift in order to accept the new location.

I use this analogy for us to understand the importance of letting go of any animosity towards others. Choosing to let go of any grudges or hard feelings offers a sense of freedom to accept what lies before us. In many cases, letting go allows us to see what's been right before our eyes but unrecognized previously. Think of situations in your life where you held on to a position that you had because you became comfortable and complacent with it. You may have been hurt the last time you posted for a new position because you gave it your all but did not get the job. You might have become gun-shy to explore new opportunities. Over the years, you've seen many others transition and wish you had made a move previously. It takes you time to get up the courage to go for what's in your heart because you have chosen to play it safe. Now, you realize that playing it safe has minimized your opportunities and personal growth potential.

It's time to let go of your past hurts, habits and hang-ups! It's time to go for what's in your heart. Be willing to receive and embrace new opportunities. Make the most of your current situation by being willing to be vulnerable enough to build new work relationships, trusting others again. It is a risky proposition but it's better to step out for what you want instead of holding on to the past so you are able to experience the best before you.

I want to conclude this chapter on letting go with words from Nina Simone's song:

Feeling Good

Birds flyin' high, you know how I feel. Sun in the sky, you know how I feel. Breeze driftin' on by, you know how I feel. It's a new dawn, it's a new day, it's a new life for me. Yeah, it's a new dawn, it's a new day, it's a new life for me, oooooooh … And I'm feelin' good.

Fish in the sea, you know how I feel. River runnin' free, you know how I feel. Blossom on the tree, you know how I feel. It's a new dawn, it's a new day, it's a new life for me. And I'm feelin' good.

Dragonfly out in the sun, you know what I mean, don't you know. Butterflies all havin' fun, you know what I mean. Sleep in peace when day is done: that's what I mean. And this old world is a new world and a bold world for me …

Stars when you shine, you know how I feel. Scent of the pine, you know how I feel. Yeah, freedom is mine, and I know how I feel. It's a new dawn, it's a new day, it's a new life for me. [scat] And I'm feelin' … good.

CHAPTER 5

Change is Good!

"When we are no longer able to change a situation, we are challenged to change ourselves."—VIKTOR E FRANKL, Author Of *Man's Search For Meaning*

DURING SOME OF MY WORKSHOPS on change management, I begin by having everyone repeat after me saying, "Change is Good!" three times. Each time we say it, we emphasize a different word. The first time we put emphasis on the word "change." The second time, we emphasize the word "is." The final time, we emphasize "good."

As an exercise, please read the following out loud: "Change is good." Now say, "Change, is Good." Finally say, "Change is, Good!"

Then I ask everyone which version they preferred and I'd like you to decide which version you prefer. Those who prefer the emphasis on the word "change" are generally okay with change. They tend to be the type who like to create change in their lives on a regular basis. Those are the ones who may switch roles every 2 years, often move, vacation abroad in different places each year.

Two companies who thrive on change are Apple and Google. Apple will create a new iPhone and not long after come out with a next generation version. Google is known to continually reinvent itself with innovative products and solutions beyond its search engine. For those of you who prefer the emphasis on the word, "is" tend to be those who don't mind the process of "change." Most people like the results of change but not what it takes to go through for that change to become their reality. As an example, many people would like to get in better shape and get to their ideal weight. They desire the change of losing weight and being in better shape, however, they don't like changing their diet or exercise routine. Those who don't mind making the adjustments of changing their routine to get what they really want are in this group. This is a unique group, but one to leverage not minding the process of change.

The final group are those who like the emphasis on the word, change. These individuals focus on the overall benefits of change. In my example of losing weight and getting on a better diet, this group focuses on having the weight loss and being in better shape. From a corporate perspective, it's the organization that analyzes the market and makes changes today in preparation for what they expect to happen in the next 2–3 years in order to remain profitable and meet the expectations of their stockholders. They're focusing on the end result of maintaining profitability in the future so they may create an organizational change today.

I use the phrase "Change is Good!" as a way for us to see the best when we experience a transition or some type of shift. Change can create a lot of anxiety for many people since it's an adjustment to the norm. Even with the most common things, with change comes natural resistance. Think about some of the things we've been wearing for years that we could easily replace but we don't. Like an old robe, slippers or sweats, many of us have been wearing the same old "inside house gear" for years because we are so accustomed to throwing it on. Not to mention how comfortable if feels on us after all these years. Despite the holes, the faded patterns, disappearing logos and the rips and tears, we continue putting it on as often as possible, whether it's clean or semi-clean.

We do this out of habit, routine and comfort. I had a pair of slippers that I wore for over 10 years and the bottoms wore out from wearing them outside to take out the trash. When I finally got a new set, I continued going to the old slippers for the first few months. The new pair were great, looked and felt nice as well. However, I had a routine and a comfort level with the old pair I wore for years. It wasn't until I threw out the old pair that I embraced the new slippers. Can you relate with a similar example? Similarly with work, letting go of previous processes, old organizational structures, previous projects, past initiatives, or perhaps last year's objectives can better allow us to embrace the new.

Change Defined

Dictionary Definitions	Over the Top Coaching Interpretations
To become different or undergo alteration	Choose who you want to be and how you want to show up. Then make the necessary adjustments to "be as you wish to seem." –SOCRATES
To undergo transformation or transition	Become a new creation. "Fire" the old you who did not perform or who was a procrastinator and begin to live to the brand new you who gets things done.
To go from one place to another	Change your environment and some of your friends and acquaintances. Get in a new place that will allow you to thrive.
To make an exchange	Exchange your poor habits for more liberating options.

How many people do you know at work who were new to a role and would constantly refer back to the way they did things in their previous group, department or company? At first, it was good to get a fresh perspective from them and their previous experience, however after being in a new position for over a year, it's time to let go of what you used to do and focus on the new environment. Like speaking of the good old days or reminiscing on how great things were back in the day. It's the old pair of slippers syndrome. It's great to leverage our past experiences but let's ensure we are looking for the good in the new situation.

When our familiar or status quo is being challenged, we tend to unconsciously resist. However, recognizing our natural tendencies is a great beginning to embrace that change is good. It's a matter of focus and perception of the change being introduced. The more we decide to find the good and focus on the benefits of the change the better and sooner we can leverage the change for our benefit.

PROACTIVE CHANGE

In most cases when the subject of change management in corporate surfaces, people tend to think about change happening to them by senior level leaders. Some examples of this type of change can be in the form of restructuring, process enhancements, acquisition or mergers, displacement of employees, leadership changes, or a combination of any of these initiatives. We generally have a reactive response since these types of changes tend to happen without input from those in middle levels of the company. It causes many to get stressed at the thought of change. Some of it is real and some is perceived as real.

As we understand our perception is our reality, I want to focus on the benefits of change so our confession can be that change is good. If we can adjust the way we perceive change, it can help the way we handle change and cause us to be more resilient as a result. The way we speak about change can also help to influence how we feel and react to change. This is where having the attitude of change being good comes in handy for us and helps us make the appropriate mental shift with corresponding actions.

Proactive is defined as action and result oriented behavior. It's a great idea to incorporate proactive change into our career strategy. This is taking into consideration what areas, if intentionally changed, would aid you in moving towards your larger aspirations. Some examples could include posting for a lateral position to expand your experiences, gain insights from a new leader and distinguish yourself from your peers. I mention posting for a lateral versus a higher level as a consideration because you may drastically improve your chances of getting to change and better position yourself for a high-level position down the road. Some overlook this approach because we tend to want to move straight up the corporate ladder as quickly as possible. Forgetting that the corporate ladder is not always a straight climb. In many cases you may jump from one ladder to another that's more stable and some steps have a larger space in between the next step. Another example of proactive change is volunteering for extra or special assignments on cross-functional teams. This can benefit your career long term with the additional experiences and key learning experiences gained.

I recall when I was working for American Express as an individual contributor in sales and my goal was to get promoted to the next level of director. There was an opportunity that came available and I posted. I gave it my best and interviewed well. The hiring manager was new to our group and decided to go with someone she previously worked with and liked. She informed me that I interviewed well and was her runner up. Instead of getting upset and focusing on the various reasons for her decision, I decided to accept it graciously and asked for her support in future opportunities.

I recall speaking with other candidates who also didn't receive the position and their responses were different than mine. They focused on the fact that she hired a previous co-worker and felt slighted. Because they felt disenfranchised, they expressed their feelings emotionally, not verbally. I'm sure you know what I mean when I say we may fake smile when we see the other person or pretend we didn't see them when we did. People typically tell on themselves by their body language.

However, I chose to focus my efforts on proactively supporting the new hire, staying in touch with that leader who chose a different candidate and not burning any bridges. As a result, when another director position became open a year later, she fully endorsed me and sent the hiring manager an email stating how receptive I was to her feedback and how I followed up with her. I ended up getting the promotion!

In order to take our career to another level it is critical to be willing to do things differently and to take the initiative to create your desired outcome. Taking an approach that your career is solely your responsibility is a great place to start because it puts us in charge of proactively managing our career. If we really want different and better results we have the choice and opportunity to change and to do so proactively. Many people that I've coached and managed make comments about their leader not totally supporting their efforts for advancement or obtaining additional responsibilities.

When I work with high achievers with a proactive approach, they tend to create a situation where they are the go-to people in their respective areas because of their can do attitude and mindset of turning lemons into lemonade. They are the ones seeking out mentors and building alliances with other leaders and high potentials. They are volunteering to participate on cross-functional teams. During meetings when the boss asks for who's willing to take on extra tasks and follow-up assignments, they're more than likely taking the initiative to do so. They are intentionally setting themselves up for opportunities. Many others take the approach of waiting for things to come their way or for their leader to volunteer them for special projects. Proactive individual contributors and managers take the bull by its horns, tackle it, tie it's feet, and conquer it in true rodeo fashion.

SYSTEMIC CHANGE

According to BusinessDictionary.com, systemic is defined as system wide, affecting or relating to a group or system—such as a body, economy or market—as a whole, instead of its individual parts. In other words, systemic change is change that is spread throughout an entire process that allows it to be long term, lasting impactful change. It's holistic change. Not just change for the sake of change but making it a regular part of what you do; a lifestyle of change.

I recall coaching some who were excited about the idea of systemic change and developed a plan of action. They did a good job of developing steps, people to contact and areas of consideration. After going down this path for a few weeks, they would run into an obstacle and eventually gave up on their strategy. They were not fully committed nor did they focus on making it a lifestyle. As an example, one individual contributor informed me of his plan to get promoted to a people leader position. I coached him on creating a plan that included identifying others in his organization to reach out to in order to develop a relationship. These were individuals who effectively transitioned from individual contributors to people leader and some were at the next level. He would see them often and would be in some meetings with them but did not approach them. He decided he would schedule lunch with them. The plan was to learn best practices and ask for mentoring. However, after a few weeks of unsuccessfully trying to get on their calendars, he decided to stop reaching out and hoped that things would just "magically" work out. He thought it was a good idea but was unwilling to persevere long term.

Another example was someone I coached who stated they were going to change their image of coming in late and doing mediocre work to someone who arrived early, stayed late, goes the extra mile so they would be a go-to person. They only lasted a few days. As soon as something personal came up and they were late, they got discouraged and said they would still over-achieve at their own pace.

Obstacles and challenges will come, but in order for systemic change to pay off, you have to anticipate the challenges and consider them part of the process, yet continue with the new plan. The idea of perseverance is sticking it out when things get tough. Based on my experience of working with many high potentials they explore new approaches and make minor adjustments that are short-term. Over a period of time they migrate back to their usual ways and end up with the same results and in many cases, remain frustrated with their situation.

It's similar to the many people who say they want to diet to lose weight. Sometimes the goal is to do it for an upcoming event like a wedding, for the summer season so they can wear a nice swimming suit at the beach or just simply because they desire to get to their ideal weight and size. The challenge with some who diet is that it's temporary. They do it for a little while and obtain temporary results. However, if they don't maintain it and make it a lifestyle, it will not be lasting.

In order for systemic change to have the long-term intended outcome, it will take making the changes a standard way of doing things. The key is to take the necessary time to let the new actions become habit forming so it's lasting.

STOP THE INSANITY

A widely quoted definition of insanity is, "doing the same things over and expecting different results." I appreciate this definition of insanity as it helps us to challenge our widely accepted way of doing and being. It relates directly to allowing us to better understand the need for change. As society and business is constantly evolving, it's critical that we take a proactive approach to not getting stuck or becoming complacent with the way things are today.

This definition fosters insight on our desire for improved outcomes and results versus the process that it requires to facilitate making it happen.

I read a great coaching book written by Marshall Goldsmith titled *What Got You Here Won't Get You There*. The book had a lot of insights, but my focus for this section is the title. I've coached and worked with many who have a great track records of success that have worked in the past. Those who continue to adjust their approach also usually continue that success. However, those who keep doing what they've done in the past can be what's described in the music industry as a "one hit wonder." They get one great song or album and that's it. I recognize that I'm sometimes guilty of acting insane.

There have been many times where I've made a commitment to myself to consistently workout over the years. At various times over the year I've been more consistent than others but I seem to go in phases. My goal has been to have a more muscular physique at my ideal weight. I've been close to my objective at various times and then I get off for short periods of time and over the years I see the difference. When I'm in the gym 3–4 times a week, running 3 times a week, doing my home routine and have a matching diet, I'm feeling and looking my best. Then something legitimate comes up that might cause me to miss a day and that turns into missing a few more. Next thing I know, I'm down to 1 day a week of running or working out and my diet quickly follows my lack of persistence. I can acknowledge this pattern but if I don't do anything different to stop it, I'll continue to experience the ups and downs. If I continue this pattern and expect to get the body I desire, then I'm insane to think I actually will. If I really want the physique, I'm going to have to change my pattern to remain consistent and keep my exercise routine and good diet habits as part of my regular lifestyle.

Similar to many that I've coached, managed, worked with and have been myself in the corporate environment who say they want to be at the top of the sales rankings or get the best year-end ratings for their role. In previous years they've been rated in the middle and have received feedback on what's expected to get better ratings. However, they continue to produce the same results, continue to work hard but not smart and their results remain just okay. Yet, because of their tenure, experience and expectations, they believe they should get higher performance ratings. Jim Rohn, the late motivational speaker and author stated, *"In order to do better, we have to become better."* It's about changing who we are to become the type of person it takes to obtain our intended results.

GET ANGRY

A great way to stop the insanity and have the drive to change is to get angry. As the saying goes, until we get sick and tired of being sick and tired, nothing changes.

I recall getting to a point of frustration with myself. I had been working in sales for 10 years since college and had desired to lead a sales team for years. I worked in a variety of industries and for various organizations with solid results. I understood in order to be considered for leadership roles in sales, I had to be one of the top performers as an individual contributor. After seeing a few peers get promoted, getting better results and positive feedback from leaders, I made a quality decision that I would do what it takes to better position myself for promotion. I was getting sick and tired of desiring a promotion and not getting any opportunities for a promotion that I was going to do everything possible to put things in order for that to happen.

I decided to have calls and meetings with those who had recently been promoted to learn from them. I let my leader know my intentions and asked for his endorsement and he obliged. I developed a strategy of targeting my largest opportunity accounts and I sold internally to get the best customer offers and build stronger relationships with my clients. As a result, I was ranked second out of about 80.

When an opportunity for the next level position became available, I posted and did not get it. However, it better positioned me for the next opportunity that I did get. This was a result of me getting angry with myself for missing out on potential opportunities for advancement. However, I had to become a more strategic person by changing my approach.

Emotions are natural for all of us as long as we know how to manage and use them to our ultimate advantage. Many coaching clients share and express their emotions over various work and life situations. You see, some professional sports coaches on television get angry about what they perceive to be a bad call by a referee. You may also notice athletes openly express their frustration with their teammates. This is a natural response to something that is not working or others feeling they're not getting a fair opportunity. Instead of not doing anything, they openly and sometimes uncontrollably lash out. When an athlete openly expresses their emotions with a referee or other players it can sometimes work to their advantage. They may not get their desired outcome immediately, but it will cause a referee to think twice about the next call or other players to step up their game. Like the saying goes, it's the squeaky wheel that gets the grease.

Getting angry can also help to create positive change in society and the world. Consider that Gandhi was angry. He was angry about oppressive taxation and discrimination of poor farmers and laborers. He struggled to alleviate poverty, liberate women and put an end to discrimination, with the ultimate objective being self-rule for India.

Martin Luther King Jr. was angry about social injustice. His leadership came into prominence as a result of Rosa Parks being angry from having to sit on the back of the bus. Their anger led to an international movement of non-violence based on Gandhi's example. This led to laws being changed, which changed our society for the good. Nelson Mandela's anger led him to helping bring an end to apartheid in South Africa. As a result of his anger being channeled in a positive direction, he became the President of South Africa and an advocate of human rights around the globe.

Another example is the organization called MADD (Mother's Against Drunk Drivers). Candy Lightner founded MADD in 1980 after her daughter, Cari, was killed by a repeat drunk driving offender. Beckie Brown established the first MADD chapter in Northern Florida when her son, Marcus Brown died at age 18 from injuries suffered in a traffic crash involving a 19-year old drunk driver. Beckie is known to have channeled her grief into action.

Controlled anger channeled in the right direction can make a positive difference for us in our careers and lives as well. Many of us should get to the point of being sick and tired of being sick and tired of the same old stuff that we become angry enough to be willing to change. In many cases this may be the best way to help us take the needed action to actually change our situation.

Based on this, I would like to challenge you to get angry. Take a moment to think about things in your career that you've been tolerating for any extended period of time. Remember that your career is your responsibility so this is not an exercise of blaming others or getting angry with others. This is an exercise in getting angry with yourself over your current situation in an effort to motivate you to change.

The results of positive change can be life changing and help you get to where you really want to be.

I think there are several points to leverage as it relates to our career. Sometimes we are too nonchalant about our career or work situation. Therefore, I want to challenge you to get angry at your situation if it's not working for you. Get angry enough at yourself for not performing at your best. The point is to be angry enough to do something different to obtain your desired results. Take full responsibility for your career and your current situation and begin to take action.

When I think of people getting really angry, I envision people throwing chairs or hitting inanimate objects as well as raising their voice with all types of words. I view that as changing our environment. Maybe we need to change our environment by throwing some bad habits out of our lives and moving some negative people out of our lives. Consider all the things and people you've been tolerating. Get angry enough to take action to change that situation to position yourself more effectively in a positive place that will foster organic change.

Organic change is internal. When companies grow, they can do it through acquiring other organizations or through expanding their business internally. In the retail industry, they use the phrase, "same store sales" to help investors better understand if the growth of a company is related to internal improvements or through external means. Both methods can help to increase earnings, however, organic growth is perceived to be a sign of a healthier organization that have working processes already in place.

On the contrary, a company who is performing poorly can

mask their internal challenges with an acquisition to give the impression of higher sales.

Another way to elaborate on the point of positive anger leading to organic change is the phrase. Systemic change. This is used in various industries with slightly different meanings. I view systemic change as making major fundamental changes. So the new change is long-term and lasts to the point where it becomes a new habit and ultimately a lifestyle.

Think about the impact of the previous examples of those who became angry about a situation and channeled it into positive action that changed nations. Their anger was their passion which fueled change for the long-term as they committed their lives to their endeavors.

As you consider what makes you angry and what actions you're going to take to change for the better, please take steps to ensure it's something that's sustainable. The stronger your passion for it, the more likely it is to become a new way of working and living.

Exercise

Answer and ponder the following questions:

1. What is it at work about yourself or your situation that gets on your nerves?
2. What would an ideal situation look like if things were changed the way you desire?
3. What is one step you can take in the next 24 hours to begin the process of changing it?

4. What will you commit to doing consistently to ensure it's long-term?

5. Who can you engage to keep you accountable? Please contact them before the end of the day.

HIRE A TURNAROUND SPECIALIST

Years ago, I read a book titled *"Mean Business: How I Save Bad Companies and Make Good Companies Great"* by Al Dunlop. He is a retired corporate executive and best known as a turn-a-round specialist and professional corporate down-sizer. There is another book written about him titled *Chainsaw Al: The Notorious Career of Al Dunlap in the Era of Profit at Any Price* by John A. Byrne. This book describes Al as being ruthless at downsizing corporations for short-term shareholder profit. According to the overview of this book on Amazon, Al was reviled on Main Street, but loved on Wall Street for bringing in huge returns for shareholders and investors.

When a company is having challenges in some cases they bring in a new leader who has a reputation as being a turn around specialist to help save the company from bleeding to making them a profit center. Or in some cases, they change things around to ensure returns to shareholders.

I recommend we do the same thing with our career. Fire the current person in charge and hire a turn around specialist. In other words, hire a new you. You can become a different person by taking a different perspective of your situation and being willing to change. Evaluate your situation and determine what it

146

would take to get the desired results. If necessary, bring in "consultants" to help you assess the situation. "Consultants" can be mentors, high performing peers or others getting the type of results you aspire to attain. As a turnaround specialist you have the freedom to fire the old staff. You may need to let go of some of your under-performing habits and team members. Think about those influencing you for the negative and the positive. Keep those who help and eliminate any distractions.

The goal is to make the necessary changes not only survive but to begin to thrive. Recognize if you're not pulling your own weight and admit it. Analyze your current situation from a third party perspective. Act as if you are a consultant hired to assess "You Incorporated." Complete the following exercise of rating your level of satisfaction in the following areas on a scale of 1–10, with 1 as not satisfied and 10 as very satisfied:

- Career
- Money
- Personal Growth
- Family/Friends
- Significant Other
- Health
- Physical Environment
- Fun/Recreation

If your level of satisfaction is less than an 8 in any of the categories then you have some work to do. The goal is to get to a 10 in all areas of your life and not settle for anything less.

As you begin to evaluate your situation be open to asking yourself if you have been giving your best effort in each area. Have you been doing enough to create and obtain your desired results in all areas? If not, then be willing to fire yourself.

By firing yourself you are giving yourself permission to admit mistakes by taking full responsibility for where you are in your life. Then choose to give yourself a fresh start, a new beginning based on making a new commitment to being and doing your best.

There is a quote by Marianne Williamson that I think helps bring the point home:

> "Our greatest fear in not that we are inadequate, but that we are powerful beyond measure. It is our light, not our darkness, that frightens us. As we are liberated from our own fear, our presence automatically liberates others ..."

In my experience and time coaching a variety of managers, I have heard some state that they are not doing or giving their best at work. They make statements around not being willing to go all out for their boss for a variety of personal reasons. However, that only limits their ability and minimizes their results. It essentially prevents them from determining what they are truly capable of doing because of their unwillingness to give their best.

I have had some clients who bring a lot to the table at work but choose not to share their thoughts. I've worked with others who did not know how best to articulate and contribute to their organization or relationships. This is why it's critical to recognize where you are and be willing to change to become new by determining the characteristics of people whom they aspire to be like. Then begin to model and exemplify similar actions to get desired results.

EMBRACE CHANGE

It's been stated that a lesson not learned will be repeated. In an effort to move to our proverbial next level, it's important for us to learn to embrace change. It can be challenging but well worth the effort. Today, working in corporate is working in an environment of constant change where things are dynamic. One period of time, the focus may be on growing and expanding. A few months later it may be about reducing costs. A few months after that, you might have a period of reorganization and another new direction that will come again. Understanding this part of the process is important. Going with the flow and choosing to adjust accordingly is more important.

Most in senior levels seem to get it and even though they may not like it, they have learned to embrace it without complaining. However, I have heard more complaining in the entry and middle levels. This does not help nor will it change anything. Those who learn to get on board faster tend to fare better in the long term.

A great strategy to embracing change is creating a sense of urgency. It's also good to keep the purpose of the change at the top of your mind. A sense of urgency assists with incorporating change as if it's something you are making a priority. Ensuring that you are walking out the commitment of the change will help with the assimilation process.

Myles Munroe stated that without understanding the purpose of a thing, abuse is inevitable. The more we keep the reasons in mind for the change and magnify its importance, the better the ability to leverage the change.

John P. Kotter wrote a popular book on change entitled, *Leading Change* that I read when I was getting my MBA. It focused on organizational change in the corporate environment and is a great reference. One of the points he highlights regarding integrating change is gaining short-term wins as an incentive to continue with the change. As you proceed to embrace change, explore what you consider a win. If you're changing your approach when working with colleagues to gain influence as you enhance your relationship, take time to acknowledge it and celebrate the accomplishment. Determine how best to leverage this win with the others you're targeting to influence. This can help keep you encouraged to continue in the process.

The following is an overview of the change process and its potential impact:

- Changed thinking leads to changed beliefs
- Changed beliefs lead to changed expectations
- Changed expectations lead to changed attitudes
- Changed attitudes lead to changed habits
- Changed habits lead to changed character
- Changed character leads to a changed destiny

I will conclude this chapter on change being good by sharing my takeaways from reading the book written by Spencer Johnson, MD, entitled *Who Moved My Cheese.* It's a fictional story that beautifully illustrates how to deal with change in a creative way by using two mice as the main characters. They represent two types of people in how they manage change. One is a complacent complainer who likes the way things are and is unwilling to adjust. The other is like someone who reads the writing on the wall as change is taking place. They are risk oriented, courageous and open to adjusting as necessary. The story essentially highlights their original pattern for obtaining cheese to eat and feed their families. However, one day the cheese is moved and the mice both act out their roles. Below is a high-level summary, but I recommend you read the book to get the full message.

For those of you who have already read the book, the below summary will resonate well with you.

- Change happens
- They keep moving the cheese
- Anticipate change
- Get ready for the cheese to move
- Monitor change
- Smell the cheese often so you know when it's getting old
- Adapt to change quickly
- The quicker you let go of old cheese, the sooner you can enjoy new cheese
- Change
- Move with the cheese

- Enjoy change!
- Savor the adventure and enjoy the taste of the new cheese
- Be ready to change quickly and enjoy it again
- They keep moving the cheese

Based on reading this chapter, what will you commit to do differently so as things happen you will be able to confidently state: *Change Is Good!*

PART 2

LEADERSHIP FOUNDATIONS

"Leadership and learning are indispensable to each other."
—JOHN F. KENNEDY

CHAPTER 6

Authentic Leadership

"Be as you wish to seem." —Socrates

According to a **2015** article in *Fortune Magazine* by Patricia Sellers, Millennials/Gen Y are expected to comprise 75% of the global workforce by 2025. This significant group values authenticity, transparency and access to power.

Authentic leadership is a popular topic in corporate today. I speak to many large corporations employee resource groups. The most requested topic that I am asked to discuss is authentic leadership. A few years ago, I was invited to speak at Clorox employee resource groups' summit and when their CEO heard I was speaking on the topic of authentic leadership he requested to provide the introduction and share his thoughts on it as well.

I define authentic leadership as being in alignment with your values, leveraging your strengths and experiences despite your environment while fostering your natural behavioral style in a position of influence. The key to leading from your authentic self is consistently being yourself regardless of your environment.

I had an opportunity of conducting a leadership workshop for a group of sales professionals at a large financial services company. One participant was naturally comical. He would make comments during the workshop that would cause everyone to laugh and others on his team mentioned how funny he was on a regular basis. However, when it was time for him to present a business exercise, he was not funny at all. I asked him what happened to his natural humor and he stated he does not use his humor when dealing with customers. I challenged him and stated it's to his advantage to maintain his humor with his clients because it's naturally who he is. I stated customers buy from people they like and trust. Remaining authentic to your natural style draws people to you.

A year later, I was hired to conduct a strategy session to that group and asked the same gentleman how he applied "who he is" to working with his clients and what the results had been. He shared with the team and me that he began being himself with his clients and integrating his humor with prospecting. As a result, he had been able to connect with his clients more effectively, had more in depth customer relationships, had taken more risk using his humor with clients and it had resulted in more business along with a promotion.

Through my experience working with corporate professionals I have heard many people state they are one way with co-workers and another way with their friends. There is a perception that you have to act a certain way that is out of natural character for many because they believe their natural leadership style may not be as acceptable as the majority in their corporate environment. As a result, many lead in a non-authentic manner. Over an extended period of time, this can cause the leader to become frustrated at attempting to lead in a way that is not in alignment with their personal values nor leveraging their strengths and experiences.

As a middle or entry level professional in a company, it's critical for your success to remain an authentic leader. You allow others the opportunity to experience someone from perhaps a different culture apply their unique style in leading in a corporate environment to drive bottom line results. It will help enhance the workplace to value diversity and for others to appreciate and leverage their uniqueness to move up the corporate ladder. Additional benefits include being in alignment with your values, gaining peace of mind from leading with integrity, and having the self-confidence to drive business results effectively through others.

I recommend taking the following steps to become an authentic leader:

- Recognize who you really are
- Position by differentiation
- Adapt, not adopt

- Demonstrate competence with self-confidence
- Be you

"Every time you suppress some part of yourself or allow others to play you small, you are in essence ignoring the owner's manual your creator gave you and destroying your design."–OPRAH WINFREY

RECOGNIZE WHO YOU REALLY ARE

I speak to many corporate employee association groups and professional business organizations on various business and leadership topics. When I talk on the topic of recognizing who you really are, many of the participants need clarification on the statement. Their thought to recognize means to become aware of something you did not previously know. Many state, "How could I not know myself since I've been myself my whole life?" This is why I use the adjective "really." Generally speaking many managers in corporate are in their current roles as a result of things just working out that way. They state how they "fell into" their current position because they always worked in a certain industry. However, there are other leaders in companies who designed their career path based on first recognizing who they really are. They went through a process of taking time to reflect and think about their interests, strengths, and unique experiences.

Through my management coaching experience I've discovered many business professionals are excellent at conducting a SWOT analysis (Strengths, Weaknesses, Opportunities, Threats)

on their corporate business, products, services, etc. They conduct market research, analyze data, and make strategic decisions based on the information gained to drive business results. However, very few have taken time to conduct a self-analysis to truly understand their personal strengths, weaknesses, opportunities, and threats.

Applying some of the same principles in the business process of learning about a product, service, or initiative to yourself will provide you with insights to help you recognize who you really are. I recommend taking the following steps:

- Obtain a self-assessment
- Conduct a values assessment
- Identify your strengths
- See yourself in your maximized state of being

OBTAIN A SELF-ASSESSMENT

Obtaining a self-assessment can be done formally through a 360-degree assessment, personality assessment, behavioral style assessments and many others. Anecdotal feedback should also be considered from family, friends, associates in your community organizations, and other personal and business connections.

Formal assessments are great tools to help you better understand your strengths, weaknesses, opportunities, and threats in your career as a manager. Most senior level executives obtain assessments regularly to help them adjust, as they deem appropriate to help make them better leaders.

In almost all of my workshops, I begin with some type of a self-assessment. The purpose is to provide the participants with a starting point, and to understand their current state in the context of the topic at hand. This allows them to understand how others perceive them, which can be very insightful.

Effective managers consider themselves to serve those they lead. Obtaining an assessment of others' perspectives can help to make appropriate adjustments based on reality versus our own personal assumptions.

Consider if you play golf or tennis and you go to a pro for lessons. What's one of the first things they'll ask you to do? They will typically ask you to hit the ball. They want to get an idea of what you can currently do. This provides them and you with an assessment of areas to focus on for improvement.

The same principles apply for the corporate professional obtaining a self-assessment.

CONDUCT A VALUES ASSESSMENT

Values are what matter most to us. Values are what we hold dear. If we live in alignment with them, we can experience deep fulfillment. They are worth orienting our lives around. A value is an enduring belief that a specific mode of conduct is personally preferable to a different one. Values are guiding principles. They are overriding beliefs in our lives with respect to the personal ends we desire. Values are standards. Values are empowering. Values allow you to be more in control of your life when they are clear and honored consistently.

Please complete the values assessment below. Circle the values below that resonate most with you. Rank how important each is to you on a scale of 1 to 5, with 1 being most important.

Achievement	Learning
Adventure	Leisure Time
Aesthetics	Love
Affection	Loyalty
Altruism	Mastery
Appearance	Meaning
Arts	Money
Authority (Power)	Openness
Autonomy/Independence	Originality
Beauty	Peace
Career	Perfection
Community	Personal Growth
Competence	Physical Health
Contentment	Pleasure
Control	Privacy/Solitude
Creativity	Recognition
Devotion	Relationship
Emotional Health	Religion
Environment	Risk Taking
Excellence	Romance
Expertise	Security
Family	Service
Freedom	Sex
Fun	Socializing
Glamour	Spirituality
Health	Status
Home	Thoughtful
Honesty	Trustworthy
Integrity	Wisdom

Now list your top five values in order of importance to you.

1. _____

2. _____

3. _____

4. _____

5. _____

Companies have discovered the benefits of listing their corporate values and sharing their guiding principles with employees. The purpose is to create a unified organization based on what matters most to the company and having everyone operate from the same foundational points.

Corporate values can be used as a barometer for determining fit with new hires, evaluating candidates for promotional opportunities, and as a factor in releasing employees. We should take the same approach with our values by using it as a litmus test for evaluating opportunities. The first question you should consider asking yourself when considering new opportunities or making decisions around whether to stay or go is, "How does this fit with my personal values?"

I recall coaching a young lady who was struggling in her sales job. The women shared how she was fired from a previous company and was having challenges in her current role. She wanted coaching regarding whether she should take another sales position with a different organization. I asked that we take a step back and evaluate her values. After a deep exploration she shared her top values were around kids, her home environment and family. Based on her values, I asked how she came to choose sales as a career. The young lady stated it was the first job she was able to get out of college and it was challenging to do something different so she just stayed with it. Based on our discussion the women realized the sales role was not in alignment with her values and we began exploring opportunities that were more in alignment with what mattered most to her. She was pleased with this analysis because her unsuccessful sales career was diminishing her confidence in her abilities to be effective in her career. She emailed me a year later to thank me for the coaching as she was now managing a day-care center which was much more fulfilling for her.

I coached an individual who worked for a tech company in Silicon Valley who explained she was content being a manager level, individual contributor because it better aligned with her values and strengths. She did not want to get into senior management because she felt the demands of senior management and leadership roles did not fit her style. Fortunately, she was able to obtain raises and new challenges as an individual contributor at the manager level.

I coach many people who are doing things outside of their values, and have complained of various challenges and frustrations. Frustration is a result of not being in alignment with your values. Once you take time to determine your top values ensure that you begin to live by them and to allow them to be your driving force.

IDENTIFY YOUR STRENGTHS

Obtaining a strength assessment can be very helpful in understanding your value to the marketplace. We learn about our history in school to learn from our past. A study of history provides us with information of things to leverage and avoid so we don't repeat the same mistakes. Similarly a great place to start to identify your strengths is by reviewing your past as it relates to major accomplishments and experiences.

Begin to reflect on your past as if you were writing a memoir for your loved ones about your past successes. Ask yourself questions based on what you loved experiencing in your past. The key word to focus on is love. I recommend that you capture this information in a personal journal. Journals are great tools that can provide you with a mode of capturing your thoughts and feelings about various experiences. As you begin to capture what's in your head on paper, it will provide you with clarity and insight.

I've been journaling for over thirteen years and it has helped me better understand my strengths. I began by capturing my thoughts and feelings about various business situations and accomplishments as they occurred. I do not write in my journal every day, I typically write when I'm inspired to do so or after an experience that I enjoyed or that made an impact to me. I go into more details about journaling in the chapter on Goal Setting Works later in this book.

As I review my journal entries, I noticed how I wrote when

I was working and gave a presentation that went really well. I'd write what happened, how I felt about it and what people said to me about it. Over a period of time, I'd begin to notice patterns, repetitive situations and comments that made me proud. It spoke volumes to me about what I loved, what people commented about my accomplishments, and my feelings about it. Based on reviewing my journal entries, I learned and obtained confirmation that my strengths are around my ability to inspire others, presentation skills, my natural curiosity in learning about others' goals and having a desire to support others in achieving their goals.

Once you have your questions answered and written in your journal, begin to evaluate all the information gathered. Be sure to include what others have stated about your strong suits. Include comments from co-workers, friends, family, and other associates to insure you're obtaining a balanced assessment.

As you go through the process of reviewing the things you love from your experiences analyze all the information and begin to write the major themes. Write out the adjectives that describe your strengths.

In my corporate team building workshops, I have teams conduct an exercise to help them uncover their strengths. I divide the group in smaller teams. In their team they have to share what they see are the strengths in their team members. In many cases people are pleasantly surprised how others positively perceive them. Sometimes we perceive ourselves in one way and others see us in another more significant way. Analyze your perception versus others and integrate the formal assessments in your evaluation. Begin to create an overall assessment of who you really are based on all the information gained.*

SEE YOURSELF IN YOUR MAXIMIZED STATE OF BEING

Write out a description of your ultimate self in your maximized state of being. Your maximized state of being is when you are living up to your potential. Your potential is what you have not done yet. One of our biggest challenges of future success can be our last success. I have coached many who are living in the past. They are reveling about the good old days and what they accomplished years ago. If we are more excited about our past rather than our future we may be in a position of complacency.

Review your accomplishments as what they truly are, past successes. Then take the attitude of a sales manager; once a sale is over, it's over. Their perspective immediately shifts to, "what's next?" What can I do to raise the stakes in order to strive for more? As an example, when I worked as a manager of national accounts, my goal was to be promoted to a sales director. I received a good performance rating the prior year. I chose to raise the bar from my previous year's results. I was already working 12-hour days and did not want to increase the hours based on my value of family; however, I did want to increase my production. I focused on two areas. One was meeting my sales objectives and the other was demonstrating leadership capabilities.

Resource: "Strength Finder 2.0" by the Gallup Organization

I decided to write out a quarterly personal action plan. As I went through this process I kept asking myself, "What else can I do." I chose to not only meet my personal sales goals but to help others on the team (my peers) do the same. I shared best practices with others by giving my peers (through my manager) copies of my strategy, customer newsletters, and sales tactics that worked for me. By the end of that year, I exceeded my sales target, was ranked second in all of North America, and was promoted to sales leader.

These results were from me first believing and perceiving myself as a leader prior to it happening. Genuine authenticity is what people are in search of. You can't trust people who are not genuine because you don't know who they'll be in any given situation.

When I talk to groups on the subject of authenticity, I ask for all the leaders in the room to raise their hands. It amazes me that typically about 50% raise their hands. My definition of a leader is a person of influence. We should all be influencing others in some capacity. If you do not consider yourself a leader then others will not perceive you as a leader. It begins with you first seeing yourself as your desire to be and you will naturally begin to walk it out in your unique way.

POSITION BY DIFFERENTIATION

I define positioning as a marketing strategy of creating a desired perception of a product or service in the market place. This may be accomplished by advertising, packaging and messaging to connect to the emotions and senses of the target audience. The benefits from a marketing perspective of effective positioning of a product or service are the following:

- An emotional connection by the end-user
- A clearly identified and recognized brand
- Perceived value
- Consumer demand
- Sales

As an authentic corporate professional, it's critical to your long-term success to position yourself by differentiating yourself. This can be done similar to the way a company positions a product. After you've completed recognizing who you really are by leveraging your strengths, identifying your core values and viewing yourself in your maximized state of being, then it's time to leverage what you've learned to distinguish yourself.

This should be a natural process based on your authentic self. The thought is to do as Socrates said, "Be as you wish to seem." The following points that I learned from Myles Munroe should help you recognize the significance of this process.

- The more rare a thing, the higher the value
- Out of 7.4 billion people on the earth no one else has your fingerprint
- We are permanently rare
- You lose your value when you imitate people
- Being yourself protects your value
- Everyone is necessary

Answer the following questions to help you position yourself by differentiating yourself:

1. Who are my heroes? Past or present people I admire.
2. What characteristics do I admire most?
3. Who are the best leaders I've personally been associated?
4. What qualities made them a great leader to me?
5. What characteristics and qualities do I bring to the table that I can identify specific examples?
6. Write out the qualities and characteristics of other heroes and leaders I admire and view my current ones.
7. Identify the gaps between what I admire and where I currently am.
8. Develop a plan of action to begin to live out the characteristics I desire to be known as.

Other points of consideration after completing the exercise to ensure you've met the following criteria:

- Be distinct or risk being extinct
- Branding is about differentiating yourself
- Getting people to see the difference is marketing
- Getting people to pay for the difference is selling

The final point of getting people to pay for the difference is the litmus test. Paying for the difference is when you get a promotion, recognition, improved results, enhanced 360 scores, increased responsibilities, etc. Then you will know that positioning by differentiating has truly paid off *(pun intended)*.

ADAPT–DON'T ADOPT

The next element of authentic leadership is to ensure that as a corporate professional, new to a position or team, you distinguish yourself in the context of your company and your role. There is a balance in the corporate environment to make sure you're not so distinct that you do become extinct because no one could connect with your uniqueness. Remember there is a code of conduct and dress in Fortune 500 companies. They allow for uniqueness but not extreme differences that may distract others from being productive.

In order to ensure a balanced approach, I recommend that you adapt instead of adopt your style. The definition of adapt is to bring one thing in correspondence or in harmony with another. Adopt is defined as accepting something created by another or foreign to one's nature.

When you join a company know that you first have to take time to get to know the culture you've joined. Then get in harmony to ensure your unique style flows with the culture. I recall a previous manager I worked for, who had been with the company for over 30 years shared how corporate changes are constant. He stated the way he thrived throughout the years was to learn to adapt his personal style to the mandate of the company. He used a dancing example. If you are in a group that is dancing to a one step beat and then senior management makes some changes that cause the corporate culture to change to a two-step beat, then adjust to the two step with your own flavor. It's similar to line dancing. Everyone is flowing together, yet many have their own style of dancing. Everyone is flowing with many different variations, yet the same move. You may move with a Caribbean flair, someone else with more of a European beat, but we're all moving to the same beat, just distinctly.

When you are promoted to a new position or joining a new team know that you are being brought on based on your uniqueness. Leaders typically hire or promote people based on what they will bring to a group that is different or that is missing. In many cases over a period of time, a new manager can lose the very reason they were hired from adopting to the new environment instead of adapting. When you adopt, you tend to blend in and end up doing the same old things as the others. Yet, the leaders who are recognized are the one's thinking and doing things differently. In many cases, they get associated with having some of the following attributes:

- Out of the box thinker
- Innovative
- Global thinker
- Solution oriented
- Effective executioner
- Results driven
- Over the top performer

As a newly hired or promoted individual contributor you will be expected to bring a fresh perspective to your role. This is an important fact to be conscious of and to be comfortable being you.

DEMONSTRATE COMPETENCE WITH CONFIDENCE

I have noticed from coaching many middle level leaders that they are constantly looking for the next position or level in their career. They ask many questions related to steps to take to help them get in a position for promotion or another role.

One of the most effective activities that can be done as a middle manager is to perform in your current position. If you consider your current role as a stepping-stone, a short-term role, or something you don't prefer, you have to first demonstrate competence where you are currently. In order to be seriously considered for a new role tomorrow you have to perform where you are today.

There are two areas of focus to support your authentic efforts where you are. One is the technical skill of your current role and the other, your leadership skills. I recommend obtaining a 360-degree feedback, obtaining insights from your leader, peers, subordinates, and in some cases, clients. Review your performance with your manager as well. The goal is to determine areas of opportunity for you to focus on leveraging and enhancing. If you identify technical skills as an area lacking, be comfortable going to the subject matter experts for help. If it's leadership skills, ask your manager for permission to take leadership programs and look for opportunities to practice the skills learned. I also recommend asking for an executive coach. The coach can help you maximize your strengths where you are today and to develop the needed skills for tomorrow.

Obtaining high performance reviews is a great way to distinguish yourself as a strong and competent leader. As you begin to excel in your current role, new and more challenging opportunities will naturally come your way. I recommend exploring new opportunities only after you have consistently mastered your current role at the 80% maximum factor. The thought is if you are at 100% of maxing out of your role, then it might be too late or more challenging. In many cases, I've seen people stay in a role so long that they get "type cast" as being only competent for their current role. There is a balance but it's important to view and interview others who had your current role to get a better indication of timing and performance levels. Traditionally, timing tends to be a little longer for the average performing manager so it will be critical to monitor your results and timing compared to others who had your role.

Be you! The essence of authentic leadership is to have the courage to be true to yourself regardless of your circumstances and situations. There are many quotes, proverbs, and clichés related to essentially remaining authentic:

- "Do you" —Russell Simmons
- "To thine own self be true" —William Shakespeare
- "As a man thinks in his heart so is he" —King Solomon
- "The Real Deal" —Evander Holyfield

In professional sports there is a lot of controversy over the use of sports enhancement drugs with professional athletes. Many are being tested to ensure authenticity to the game or competition is intact. Otherwise, the integrity of the game or competition is at risk.

As an individual contributor in a Fortune 500 organization it is critical to live and work authentically. It causes you to be happier and more fulfilled in life and in business.

Consider Coach Tony Dungy who took the Indianapolis Colts to the 2007 Super Bowl and won. In my workshops on authentic leadership I used to put up a picture of Tony Dungy and ask the group who he is. The majority recognized him. I then ask what qualities or characteristics come to mind when you see or think of Tony Dungy. Typical responses are:

- Integrity
- Authentic
- Genuine
- Honest
- Leader

We normally have a discussion of how Tony Dungy remained true to his values and coaching style. A typical football coach is known to be loud, in your face, and demanding. However, Tony Dungy was known to be soft spoken yet direct and commanding. Tony could have adjusted his style when he became a head football coach in the NFL, but chose to remain true to his style and it's what worked for him.

Remaining authentic despite our differences is what will work for all of us as well. It's a choice and a decision that pays huge dividends. It caused Tony Dungy to win the Super Bowl, yet have the respect of his family, team and associates.

I have the opportunity to speak to hundreds of professionals at Fortune 500 companies who state remaining authentic throughout their career has allowed them to perform better over the long term because of their consistent approach regardless of their business circumstances. Their managers, peers, and subordinates may not always agree with their way of solving business problems, yet they respect the diverse styles that produce the bottom line results.

I recommend that you spend quality time reviewing and implementing all the steps on becoming an authentic leader. Remember this is a process of recognizing who you really are, positioning yourself to be distinguished, adapting your style to flow with the group or team instead of adopting it, demonstrating competence with confidence, and to simply have the courage to be you despite your environment or circumstances. The benefits will provide you with an inner peace and a fulfilled career.

ACTION PLAN

As a result of reading this chapter please answer the following questions.

1. What will I do differently to consistently demonstrate authenticity as a manager?

2. What is my personal brand?

3. How will I enhance my uniqueness?

4. What will I do to leverage my distinctions?

5. How will I support others in remaining authentic?

CHAPTER 7

Learn To Present As If Your Career Depends On It (Because It Does!)

"Proper planning and preparation prevents poor performance."
—STEPHEN KEAGUE

I N THE BOOK *Good is Not Enough* written by Keith Wyche (who is a former CEO of ACME) with Sonia Alleyne cites that in June 2006 members of the Executive Leadership Council revisited a study they conducted in 1991. Fifty of the ELC's members were interviewed in an effort to create a "blueprint for success." These executives, who held positions of president, vice president, general managers and directors within their companies, shared their thoughts and insights on everything from indicators of success to the forces that impact success. The group not only identified communication skills as the primary skill one must master to become successful, but also gave insights into how interpersonal communication skills help tremendously in building consensus. While this study focused on minorities, I believe this applies to all entry and middle level individual contributors and managers.

One of the ways I obtained business as a corporate trainer and professional speaker was conducting lunch and learn workshops to various employee resource groups also known as ERGs. I targeted large corporations in the Bay area near my home where I already had contacts. Based on taking surveys of the ERGs, I learned that business communication skills were the number one request out of all the leadership development topics I listed. It let me know this is perceived as the most important leadership skill and the broadest topic. I understand effective business communication skills are one of the most sought after skills by hiring managers and I'm sure you've noticed it's on a lot of job postings.

The phrase "communication skills" is used a lot in business and sometimes when phrases are used a lot it can lose its impact and we can get away from its significance. The phrase I'm using for this chapter *(learn to present as if your career depends on it—because it does)* is to help in this regard. My goal is for you to understand this is not a "nice to have" leadership quality. Most everyone feels that this is an easy check mark to say he or she possesses this skill of effective communication skills because they know how to talk and have two ears to hear what others are saying.

I define effective business communication skills as the ability to convey information in a clear and concise manner to ensure the message is understood and received as intended. It also has aspects in oral and written presentation, listening, reading body language, asking and responding to questions, making requests, interpreting instructions and being empathetic. The better you are at doing these types of things effectively, the more impact you can make in your career and life. However, effective communication skills are a long-term proposition. It's something you have to constantly fine tune and update.

I enjoyed taking speech, public speaking and communications classes in school and college. However, leveraging it in a corporate environment is another story. Once I got in corporate I recognized that I needed to work on improving my ability to communicate orally and in writing. Areas I had to initially work on were being more concise, articulating my words and improving my business writing. My first leader outside of college did me the favor of providing the feedback of areas that I needed to work on improving. I didn't take offense but took advantage of the company's willingness to support my development. I first took voice lessons to help with my articulation. I later joined Toastmasters International. The organization dedicated to helping professionals improve their communication and leadership skills. As a result of my proactive efforts, my weakness became my strength and I later began to receive accolades for my ability to communicate effectively. I didn't stop my development, I continued in Toastmasters and began competing in speech contests and later was asked to represent my company in speaking at community events.

I took the Strengthfinder 2.0 assessment and confirmed this was not only an area of strength but also an area of passion for me. I later decided to continue leveraging this strength and decided to work for a training company that allowed me to become certified in training all levels of business professionals including the C-level. I trained leaders in Fortune 500 companies effective business communication skills with an emphasis on presentations. This ultimately led to me having my own training, coaching and speaking business.

The, "Learn to present as if your career depends on it - because it does," lunch and learn workshop always receives high evaluation scores. I would teach foundational principles up front and then ask for a volunteer from the audience. First, I have the volunteer speak for 60 seconds as they normally do. Then for the next 30 minutes or so, I train the volunteer on a few skills that make an impact. After I have taught them the new skills, I have them speak for another 60 seconds and allow the audience to provide their observations. The person seems to be a different person as the audience makes comments of how they first appeared when they spoke compared to how much more impactful they came across after applying the skills I taught them. I will now walk you through my transformational process.

THE IMPACT OF COMMUNICATION

There was a study by Professor Albert Mehrabian and the colleagues at the University of California, Los Angeles on human communication patterns. It essentially provided the following information that is now debated on its accuracy but I'm using it because I think it brings out a good point for consideration. The impact of communication is primarily based on your appearance (57%) when presenting, (38%) on how you sound when presenting and just (7%) on what you say. Wow!

Most people I know in corporate who have to give a presentation normally spend the majority of their time preparing the content versus the oral presentation. Another way of looking at this is to think about any good speakers you may have heard who comes to mind. It could be in business or your personal life. Think about how much you recall from the content of their discussion versus how they made you feel when they spoke. Have you ever had someone tell you about a great presentation, message, or speech they heard and say something like, "You should have been there to hear this great presentation, it was really good." And your response, "What did they say?" Their response was, "I don't know, it was just good, you had to be there to get it." This is an example of how we as receivers of communication are impacted by listening to who and what we consider to be great presenters. As the old saying goes, *It's not what you say but how you say it!* We may use words to describe what we consider to be great speakers as charismatic, charming, engaging, motivating, etc.

181

In the U.S. there are several presidents who had/have a reputation as being great orators. The top 3 that come to my mind are Presidents John F. Kennedy, Ronald Reagan and Barack Obama. They all had a way of engaging and relating to their audiences. President JFK is known to have said, "Ask not what your country can do for you but ask what you can do for your country." President Ronald Reagan is known to have been the "Great Communicator." President Barack Obama gained national recognition as a presidential contender when he, as the senator from Illinois, gave the key-note address at the 2004 Democratic National convention.

According to an article written by Richard Greene of the *Huffington Post,* "President Barack Obama knows how to work an audience. No president has ever been able to use rhythm, body language, pauses and punctuation and nuances in voice tone to "sing" a speech like Dr. King ... but at his best Barack Obama comes closest. He has the capacity to play an audience as if it were part of his own personal orchestra and that is a level of mastery that few ever reach."

The article goes on to state, "Barack Obama uses all "4 Languages" of human communication to deliver his best speeches. This is very rare and one of the biggest things that separates the top 3 from the second tier and great speakers from good ones. It is the ability to excite an audience with energy, ("Visual Language"), give them a compelling story line to follow ("Auditory Language"), rest their anxieties as you show an unshakable grasp of the facts, details and nuances, ("Auditory Digital Language") and, most importantly, to connect with, touch, move and inspire one's audience ("Kinesthetic Language").

These are examples to help demonstrate the difference it makes for those who are great communicators versus those who aren't as strong. Effective communication is and can also be a great differentiator in the corporate environment and is critical to our success. Think about the following quotes on the impact of communication skills by three great business leaders.

> • "Developing excellent communication skills is absolutely essential to effective leadership. The leader must be able to share knowledge and ideas to transmit a sense of urgency and enthusiasm to others. If a leader can't get a message across clearly and motivate others to act on it, then having a message doesn't even matter." –GILBERT AMELIO, *President/CEO of National Semiconductor Corp.*

My take-a-way: Everyone needs to improve on their ability to get a message across succinctly that causes others to take action. Otherwise, it's like the old saying "If you don't have anything good to say, then don't say anything."

> • "It takes 20 years to build a reputation and five minutes to ruin it. If you think about that, you'll do things differently." –WARREN BUFFETT, *CEO of Berkshire Hathaway*

My take-a-way: We could have taken years to build a great self-brand but all that can go out the door if we give a poor presentation to a VIP. The way we present leaves an impression—good or bad.

> • "You can have brilliant ideas, but if you can't get them across, your ideas won't get you anywhere." —LEE IACOCCA, *former CEO of Ford and Chrysler*

My take-a-way: You can have an Ivy League MBA and the alphabet behind your name but if you cannot communicate your ideas effectively, you could come across as unintelligent.

EFFECTIVE BUSINESS PRESENTATIONS

There was a study described in *The Book of Lists* by David Wallechinsky. The study says a team of researchers asked 3,000 Americans the question "What are you most afraid of?" It's unscientific because they did not provide a list to allow people to write their responses. However, it's been used for years as a reference to what people fear the most. Below is the list in order of the most popular responses:

1. Speaking before a group
2. Heights
3. Insects and bugs
4. Financial problems
5. Deep water
6. Sickness
7. Death

8. Flying

9. Loneliness

10. Dogs

11. Driving/Riding in a car

12. Darkness

13. Elevators

14. Escalators

Speaking before a group of people came out to be number one. This was surprising to me that more people who took this survey put public speaking as something they fear than others. I would have thought death would have been the most popular response or sickness or financial problems. I thought it was interesting that death was ranked 7 out of 14. When you think of what you fear the most, what comes to mind? More importantly, what are you doing to address the concern?

If public speaking is one of your biggest fears then stay tuned because help is on its way.

As I think about what makes many people nervous or anxious regarding public speaking, I believe it has to do with having the attention of an entire room of people all on you. As I've discussed this during workshops that I've led, some of the responses I'll get is people are concerned they may lose their train of thought or forget a good point and be humiliated.

This news can be comforting for some—this is normal and you are not alone. If you feel any anxiety around the thought of getting up before your peers, boss, customers and senior levels know that you have company. This is a popular response and feeling for most. In some cases, we call it butterflies in the stomach. Some get up and it's obvious to the audience as we can see them shaking, sweating profusely, knees wobbling and hands with goose bumps all over them.

No need to fear, because help is here. I have some suggestions to help you to get those butterflies to fly in formation. Tested and tried recommendations to help you turn your fear into rocket fuel to help propel you to manage your nervousness and channel it into positive energy. The following provides suggestions to help you with your impact when communicating. I will share recommendations to help you enhance your impact when communicating while doing business presentations for work.

I am going to have you record yourself while speaking to evaluate yourself. However, I'd like to begin by having a coworker that you trust and have a solid relationship with provide you with their honest observations. This is an important first step, as it will allow you to gain insight into how you're perceived by others when presenting. Most of us have assumptions about how we are viewed when presenting but it might not be totally accurate and getting others to share can be very helpful. A great first step in personal development is being aware of our current status. After that awareness we can adjust as necessary based on our objectives.

I would like for you to take a moment to prepare to have your chosen partner record you speaking on your smart phone. Plan to have them record you for 60 to 90 seconds. Think about a subject you can speak on easily for at least 60 seconds. Start by introducing yourself and state how you'd like to be perceived when presenting at work. Talk about something interesting going on at work or home. Speak for one minute as you usually would speak at work. Please only do one recording of you speaking. It's important that this is natural, like you normally would speak at work. This is to allow you to be able to have a recording of yourself speaking before going through some of my recommendations. After you practice my tips, I would like for you to do a second recording to be able to compare the two recordings. If all goes well as I expect, you should see a positive difference in your talk before and after recordings.

Please review your recording and answer the following questions based on your observation of your 60 to 90 second recorded talk. Also, have your partner share his or her observations based on the following questions and capture them in writing in your journal.

Observations on your talk No. 1:

- What did you notice about your eyes when speaking?
  – Where were you looking?
  – Were you glancing, staring, scanning, etc?
- What did you do with your hands?
  – Where were they?
  – Did you move them and if so in what way?
- What about your stance?
  – Were you standing in place or moving around?
  – Describe exactly what you noticed.

- How loud were you speaking (on a scale of 1-10 with 1 being very low and 10 being very loud)?
- Were you speaking fast, slow or moderately?
- Did your voice fluctuate or stay pretty much the same?
- Did you notice any non-words (i.e., ums, ahs, repetitive phrases or non-words)?
- Other general observations?

We will now transition to practice presentation skills based on the two main areas that impact how we are perceived when presenting. How we look and how we sound.

PHYSICAL PRESENTATION SKILLS

We discussed that most people get nervous at the thought of speaking before a group. The area I'll begin with is on eye contact. This area can have the greatest impact on helping to manage nervousness and leveraging it to your advantage when speaking. Eye contact is also one of the best areas of presentation skills that allow you to gain insight into your audience for you to adjust as necessary. Eye contact also conveys confidence by the speaker.

Eye Contact

Look at people in your audience directly. Ideally, you would look for about 3 to 5 seconds or enough time to give a thought to one person. You can adjust depending on the size of your audience. Presenting to small groups of less than 10 people will allow you to look at each person in the room. The configuration of the room you're presenting in will be a determining factor for how you adjust as well. The goal is to look at various people in different sections or parts of the room to cover the entire room. You should be looking directly in their eyes and holding it for 3 to 5 seconds. The goal is to have a one on one talk to as many people in the audience as possible. Initially, it might feel awkward but keep working on it until it feels natural.

I took a lot of public speaking classes throughout my life. My earliest memory was a public speaking class in high school where I was first introduced to this concept at a high level. I was also a member of a church during my high school years that allowed me to practice standing and speaking before others. This helped to develop my confidence with public speaking and gave me a comfort level with it so I was better equipped to manage my nervousness.

Another introduction I recall about public speaking when I was a youth was my parents teaching me to look people in their eyes when I would speak to them or when they would speak to me. They used to tell me it was a sign of respect for others and to receive it myself. I remember hearing the importance of paying attention in school to my teachers by focusing on them with my eyes. The more I focused on what they were saying and doing the better I could understand the subject being taught. However, there were times where I would be easily distracted by other students, looking at something interesting out the window or simply day dreaming. As I continued taking public speaking classes in college, getting involved in Toastmasters International and taking other public speaking classes, workshops and seminars I'd hear this same concept about eye contact. However, I would sparingly do it until one day it clicked and I made it a natural part of my speaking style. The more natural it became, the more comments I'd receive from others about my ability to connect with my audience and influence them.

It's the same concept at work when speaking in front of others, but actually doing it while speaking before a group. Literally practice looking at others for 3 to 5 seconds when speaking. Focus on giving one thought to one person. You may practice doing this while alone or if you can round up others feel free to leverage them. I'd like you to take time now to practice your previous speech and you may repeat it over to have enough time to practice these strategies. Stand up and look at 6 different people (imaginary or real) sitting in 6 different sections of the room. Front left, back right, back center, front right, back left, front center and repeat to a different person in each segment throughout the length of your talk. Get a friend or someone to record you after you practice it at least 3 different times. Remember, this is a new skill you're learning to practice and it normally starts out feeling mechanical. However, after practice and consistent use, it becomes a natural part of what you do when speaking.

Stance

Stance is your posture and body positioning while standing when presenting. This is a critical component of the 55% of the impact of your presentation in business. Think about others you've seen at work deliver stand up presentations and you notice something about their stance that was distracting or not as professional. Regardless of the content it could distract from their message or give the indication of them not being as credible simply based on how they were standing or positioned their body when presenting. Pacing, swaying, legs crossed while standing, knees buckling, legs apart or legs so close together that you're wondering if they'll fall over should the wind blow just strong enough are all indications of a poor stance.

Posture is important not just for appearance but also for proper blood flow. Facilitation of breathing enhances proper back support and improves your ability to focus. There are a variety of areas that impact posture beyond stance. It's also how we sit, type, hold our heads and carry ourselves physically. Stretching, exercising, leveraging yoga and all things that help us to enhance our postures for the long term benefits. All these areas can impact our stance and ultimately our ability to look and be our best when presenting.

When giving standing presentations, I recommend you stand with your legs about shoulder or waist width apart, without locking your knees. It should be more like an athletic stance without being slouched over. This would be your neutral position for presenting. It's totally okay to move around and to walk based on the amount of space available. However, be careful not to be distracting by pacing or making any fast movements. If you're a walker just remember to stop and make a point. Depending on space you also don't want to lock into place without any flexibility or movement as appropriate. Standing with your legs shoulder width apart and knees flexible should allow you to move naturally as appropriate based on your presentation. If you're presenting on a topic that's exciting and you have room to move, it's appropriate to flow with your talk.

I like to walk when I give standing presentations, of course depending on the room configuration. If there is room to walk around, I'm doing it purposefully and leveraging the use of effective eye contact as we discussed. I like standing close to the front row and looking people directly in the eyes closely which helps draw them in. This gesture also creates more of an intimate environment and gives those in the audience the impression that it's just a matter of time before I come their way. When I walk, I walk slowly, yet deliberately and stop to make a point as I look into someone's eyes. I enjoy leveraging the stance component of the physical presentation skills.

Gestures

Hand and arm movements when presenting in business is just as important as the other skills. This one can help enhance the delivery of your talk or distract from it depending on your proper use of gestures. There are a lot of examples of very well known politicians and business leaders using gestures both properly and improperly. There are many questions around what's appropriate to do with our arms and hands when presenting. Should we hide them in our pockets or maybe just one to give a cooler look? Is it okay to fold our arms when presenting before a group?

What about clasping our fingers together or holding our hands in front of us or behind our back?

I recommend that you allow your arms and hands to rest naturally at your sides. Gesturing should not be forced or contrived but rather be a natural extension of your talk. They should enhance your message as you move and speak. The idea is to have them at your sides as a neutral starting point and a safe place to always return. There is a balance in gesturing, as I'm sure we've all seen people who literally speak with their hands. Meaning every sentence comes with arms flying around, describing everything in non-verbal communication with their hands. The goal is to gesture as appropriate to enhance a thought or point during your presentation. There are some types of presentations that may naturally cause more gesturing than others but it will often depend on the presentation topic. Advanced speakers incorporate one-handed gestures as they are flowing with their presentation. I'd rather we focus on starting with the basics of speaking with hands at sides then incorporating the gestures as appropriate.

My approach to gesturing is making them in proportion to the size of my audience. If I'm presenting to a large group of people then I'll use large gestures. If it's a small group I'll minimize them and maybe keep them in front of my body versus expanding my arms as if I'm non-verbally describing the planet earth or something similar. Sometimes, people think these particular gestures shouldn't be used in business presentations, but I disagree. You can use gestures in one on one discussions sitting at a table with just two seats. It's simply allowing your body to do what it naturally does when speaking, especially when we are passionate about the topic at hand!

Let's test it out. Think of something that you care about or means a lot to you. Or think of a physical activity you did like a sport or attending some type of game or exercise that you really enjoyed. Take a moment and describe it out loud starting with your hands at your sides and see what happens. I like to run on trails so my story would be about describing a run and as I do, my arms naturally want to come into the running position to aid in my description. Most of us are wired to do the same. I recognize that certain cultures use gestures a lot more than others, thus it might come more natural for some than others. If you are from a culture that gestures a lot, then there may need to be a limit to the amount of gestures as to not appear out of control. The goal is balance so that it's enhancing your presentation and not distracting from it.

Voice Projection

Your ability to command attention and respect when presenting before a group is also based on your ability to project your voice. Good posture and eye contact go hand in hand with helping you to properly project your voice. However, all these critical success factors for effective business presentations take practice and focused effort to integrate into your natural style. The idea is for you to come across authentically you.

One of the best things we can do to have a successful presentation is to be ourselves when speaking before a group at work. I've had the opportunity of training many corporate leaders in business presentation skills and one of the areas I've noticed many struggle with is assuming a different character when presenting to others. They try to present like they've seen other senior leaders (whether good or bad) or how they think others expect them to present. The best way to be as impactful as possible is to present as if you're talking to friends in a professional environment. It will help you reduce nervousness and will allow you to think on your feet and be spontaneous if necessary.

When you feel comfortable with the audience, believe they are in support of your message and they want you to succeed. The idea is to take that attitude when presenting and you will do great. Incorporating all the skills you just read and practiced.

Voice projection is about being heard when speaking and in order to do so effectively, I recommend that you consider speaking a little louder than your normal speaking voice. How loud will depend on you and the audience. However, speaking in a volume around 7 on a scale from 1–10, with 1 being the lowest and 10 the highest, should be the target. This will command the audience's attention and intrigue them at the very beginning.

The best way to increase your volume when speaking and maintain a smooth resonate speaking voice is through breathing. I know we all have to breathe to live, but sometimes when we get nervous our breathing can become shallow and our speaking voice may sound squeaky or scratchy. Increasing the volume to this type of voice could be disastrous when speaking. Ideally, we want to increase the volume and keep our voice sounding normal. Voice coaches can provide more detail in this area but the main thing is to breathe normally and be okay with pausing. This helps to keep a strong speaking voice that will both get, and maintain your audiences' attention.

Pace

In order to keep the audience attention that you initially obtained from your voice projection, you will need to vary your pace throughout your talk. Pace is the speed at which you go through your presentation and it will vary on a number of factors including time allotted, people in the room, expectations, material covered and company culture to name a few.

Consider that most people like to be entertained. Understanding the focus of this is on business presentations. However, you can make a business presentation entertaining on how you choose to deliver your talk and in leveraging these tools I'm providing. I like to look at doing a presentation like a roller coaster ride. You will have your ups and downs, fast speeds, pauses and slow speeds. The variation adds to the enjoyment of the ride. It's the same idea when giving a business presentation. You can add a little spice to your presentation delivery and adjust your pace throughout your talk.

The target would be a moderate pace, but you should adjust to emphasize certain points or dig deeper in an area of audience interest. As an example, if giving a sales presentation, you may slow down on the financial offer section and speed up on the history of the company. Again the goal is to vary the pace as you see appropriate to help maintain attention throughout your entire presentation.

Inflection

When I mention inflection, I'm referring to your tone, pitch and cadence of your talk. It also incorporates your rate of speech when presenting. I also like to describe it as how we modulate or articulate our words and their flow when speaking. Do we come across in a monotone manner or more varied? If we were driving in a car and could explain our inflection would it be considered driving on a straight road, a hilly road, a bumping road or a combination of all the above?

My first corporate job after I graduated from college had me take voice lessons from a company that specialized in helping business professionals improve their ability to inflect, project their voice, articulate and speak more diaphragmatically. I recall doing a lot of breathing exercises and things to help me speak from my stomach instead of my throat. They had me practicing various sentence structures to help improve my ability to properly pronounce each word in a sentence.

I learned how to slow down and pause to articulate my points and do it in a manner that had my voice sounding rich and resonate. It was very helpful for me to leverage in work and in business. It let me know that there are little things we can do to help us make a bigger impact on our ability to present more effectively at work.

A great idea to help improve inflection is to listen to your speech a few times. Listen not only to the content, but also to your voice and how it sounds. Focus on your pace, your ups and downs and any squeaky sounds. Do you sound monotone? This provides you with insights on areas of focus to improve your inflection and your overall delivery. Your voice is your equipment and managing it to your advantage will give you a competitive advantage during your next business presentation.

Non-Words

I'm including non-words as an area of focus to improve your business presentation skills primarily because this is a big area of opportunity to many. Most use non-words unconsciously because as a result of being nervous or out of habit. Non-words are the repetitive phrases we may use such as *at the end of the day, are you with me, so* ... and many others. They also include ums, ahs, umhums, erra, hmm and other sounds that are not real words. In some organizations, many use acronyms to the extent where they can be considered non-words, but this also depends on your audience.

One of the best ways to overcome non-words is to pause in between sentences. We may have subconsciously learned from watching television or listening to the radio to minimize our gaps when presenting. Broadcasting over the radio or television is focused on not having any dead air or space so they don't miss any viewers or listeners who may tune in to their station. However, when giving a presentation it is totally acceptable to pause and have a few seconds of "dead air time." Many are not as comfortable with pausing in spite of the benefits. Pausing during a presentation can add impact if done intentionally and at the right moments. Think about a marketer using a pause effectively as they are about to announce a new ad or product. It can almost be the drum roll effect of announcing a winner of a prize. Pausing can also benefit the speaker and the audience. It allows the presenter to collect their thoughts and can aid the audience in catching up with the speaker. It allows time for pondering the topic at hand.

The goal is to eliminate all non-words from your presentations since they can take away from your 38% impact of how you sound. This can be accomplished with a focused effort of implementing pauses instead. Non-words tend to be fillers to allow us more time typically to remember our next thought or it can be done during times of transitioning or responding to audience questions. Listen to your speech to discover what your non-words are and I challenge you to practice substituting your ums and ahs with pauses and watch your presentations begin to be much more powerful.

Practice

Now that we've highlighted the major physical components of learning to present as if your career depends on it—because it does, it's time to record yourself practicing the new skills. Ask your friend who recorded you the first time to do the same after you've had a few practice runs. This time I want you to create a

5-minute presentation to allow you more time to implement all the skills. You may use a recent presentation you gave at work or one that you're currently working on. You can also make it a personal story about your work experience and your future career goals.

First, I would like you to practice just using the eye contact strategy we discussed. Decide where in the room you will begin to look for eye contact. Think about your pattern for looking at (imaginary or real) people in the room. Remember, to give one thought to one person and try to make it like a one on one conversation with a friend in a business environment.

Second, I'd like you to practice using vocal variety. This will cover voice projection, inflection and rate of speech. Think about where you want to begin your voice level and incorporate your rate of speech as well as pauses. It might seem like a lot to remember initially so take your time and feel free to focus on one area at a time until it comes out smooth.

Only after you have practiced eye contact and vocal variety would I like you to put it all together into a 5-minute presentation. Now, I would like you to have your friend record your talk so you may compare it with your initial presentation before learning these effective business presentation strategies. You may use this recording to watch and gain insights into areas of continued focus for improvement going forward.

Once you complete your recording, answer the initial evaluation based on this talk. Then compare the two presentations. The initial one and the one you just completed.

Things That Can Negatively Impact
Your Communication

How you Look (55%)	How you Sound (38%)
Dressing below your audience, disheveled, distracting colors	Using diminishing words like: I'm sorry, I'm not good at, I can't, maybe
Poor posture, shoulders down, head down, eyes looking up and down and not at your audience	Poor projection, monotone, low talker, fast talker
Timid, nervous, distracted	Reading complete sentences on slides

All these physical presentation skills require much practice and patience. As you begin using the various recommendations, be prepared to give yourself time to allow them to become a natural part of your business presentations. If you hear yourself using non-words or forgetting to use voice projection or not remembering to look at your audience, don't get discouraged. Remember it's part of the process. Don't beat yourself up and don't give up working on integrating it. Soon you will realize the non-words are going away, your gestures are naturally happening, and your breathing/pausing is allowing you to manage the nervousness. You are now equipped to be one of the best presenters in your company! Don't forget to help someone else by passing along this book to them.

PRESENTATION APPLICATIONS

There are many applications for using these skills at work. During interviews, PowerPoint presentations and presenting over the phone are just a few.

Interviews

Interviews can be high stress situations and the more prepared you are, the better. Most focus their efforts on doing the research about the company and the people. Polishing up your resume is another time-consuming activity. However, preparing for the physical components of the interview should be included and practiced with a friend. Since the format of interviews can vary from one on ones to panels, it's best to be prepared by practicing anticipated questions, your responses and having prepared questions for the interviewer(s).

Taking deep breaths can be a relaxation technique just before you walk in the room or begin to speak. The recommendations for eye contact totally apply to the interview regardless if it's one on one or more than five. It's important to give one thought to one person and to take your time and speak to each interviewer. If it's just one person then relax your gaze, but maintain eye contact. Most interviews would be from a seated position so you may not be concerned about your stance. However, you should sit in your chair with a slight lean forward with your arms on top of the table. I do not recommend sitting back in your chair with your legs crossed. I think it gives an impression that you may not be as engaged or taking this as serious as you should. Your neutral hand and arm position is on top of the table and you can gesture naturally as appropriate for the environment.

Leverage your ability to project your voice and speak from your stomach so your voice comes across authoritative to command attention and respect. Interject stories about your accomplishments to draw in those interviewing by giving them specific examples to their questions. Ensure you answer their questions directly relative to your experiences. Keep your responses concise and elaborate as they ask you additional questions about your response. Demonstrate your ability to articulate, vary your pace and demonstrate your passion about your wins and intentions. Let them get to know you personally by being authentic and share a few personal highlights about yourself and interests. They are not only looking for your relevant experiences but are also trying to determine if you would be a good fit based on if they could see themselves working with you. These basic foundations of effective business presentation skills will make a difference and help you to stand out from the crowd.

Presenting with PowerPoint slides

When giving a presentation at work with PowerPoint slides, I recommend you leverage using an LCD projector to have the information on a screen. If it's less than 3 people, you may present from your laptop, iPad or hard copy slides. When using the screen, I recommend you stand to the left of the screen as we read from left to right. When you place a slide up, make sure you introduce the slide before going into it. I do not recommend you read every point on the slide. I suggest you let the audience know what's on the slide and which points you will discuss. During your introduction of that slide you should include a summary statement the covers all the bullets on the slide. You elaborate on one or two of the bullets to help provide perspective. Always remember that PowerPoint is a visual aid tool. You are the messenger not PowerPoint. Ideally, you want all eyes on you in order to maintain control and keep attention where you want it to be.

The following is an example of how I would cover the slide below:

Business Presentation Skills

➢Applications

   ✓Presenting with PowerPoint slides

   ✓Presenting over the phone

   ✓Presenting during job interviews

There are a variety of applications for leveraging the business presentation skills we discussed. On this slide I will discuss what I consider to be the top three applications for using business presentation skills at work. The first is presenting with slides, second is presenting over the phone and thirdly, presenting during job interviews. Check out the photo on the slide. Let me know your observations based on what we discussed about effective business presentation skills. This photo is an example of presenting with PowerPoint slides and there are some things the presenter is doing correctly and a few I see he is not doing properly. (Allow time for audience interaction).

When presenting before a group with PowerPoint slides you should stand to the left of the screen. Continue using eye contact we discussed and remember to not talk to a screen but always a person. It's fine to look at the screen and point things out but when you speak about it, look at a person and then speak.

For presenting over the phone a few recommendations is to keep a list in front of you of who's on the call. The amount of people will determine the amount of interaction you may allow. Ideally, it's great to include audience interaction but you have to control it.

As the speaker, whether face to face or speaking virtually, it's important that you maintain control. The most popular type of presenting I've done in corporate was leading a team of nine managers and support staff during our weekly team calls. I'd always send the agenda in advance of the call and take roll at the beginning of each call. I'd be sure to place others on the agenda for speaking parts so it's not all on me. I prefer to make it interactive by keeping a tally of who has spoken or commented and I'll call on others who have yet to speak. I always wrap it up by summarizing the call and concluding with next steps.

Presenting during an interview is an opportunity to showcase your communications skills as well as highlight your accomplishments. Knowing that the interview gives you a chance to model your ability to communicate effectively, it's important to make the most of this opportunity by preparing and practicing in advance. It's a great idea to begin with a smile on your face and briefly with some appropriate casual conversation-but limit it to a few seconds. Manage your time to your advantage by keeping your responses concise and simple. Ensure you're understood and you answer the questions fully.

Leveraging your business presentation skills can help you maximize opportunities at work when presenting with PowerPoint slides, over the phone and during job interviews. There are other applications for using the skills and the strategies shared are transferable to all of them. What I shared are the foundational basics for effective business presentation skills. Continue to work on improving them, asking for feedback and conducting self-assessments of your presentation skills. Over time, these skills will become career-enhancing moves that will help you to stand out from the crowd.

Executive Presence

"Too little confidence, and you're unable to act; too much confidence, and you're unable to hear." —JOHN MAEDA

HOW WOULD YOU FEEL if there was a meeting that was held by your work group in which you were not invited and the focus was to discuss their perception of you? What if you were a fly on the wall and saw they put a big photo of you on the screen and began sharing their thoughts of you. What do you think your co-workers, your leader, direct reports and others you work with regularly would say?

These types of meetings happen all the time in corporate. While working as a leader in a Fortune 100 company, we would be required to assess our team members and then we would place their picture on a slide and have a discussion about them with other leaders in the organization. It would allow us leaders to assess and "rank" those in the same position. We would evaluate them on a number of factors beyond their performance to goal. We would also share our thoughts and gain insight from others on how we perceived their upward mobility and leadership capacity. This essentially boiled down to how we viewed their executive presence.

Executive presence goes beyond walking with a pep in your step, meeting goals and corporate objectives. As a people leader, I have seen plenty of individuals who could exceed their individual goals but had very low leadership qualities. They were all about themselves, would only talk about themselves and would view every initiative from the perspective of their world and did not necessarily get the big picture. Their personality was cold towards others and they were known primarily as a lone ranger. They could meet their goals as an individual contributor but if you made them a leader, they would drive away an entire team of high potential or seasoned employees.

According to a new study by the Center for Talent Innovation, a non-profit research organization in New York, being perceived as leadership material is essential to being promoted into leadership positions. In fact, the 268 senior executives surveyed said "executive presence" counts for 26% of what it takes to get promoted. Kristie Hedges states executive presence is the intersection of outward influencing skills and internal mental conditioning.

I define executive presence as a person's genuine self-confidence and ability to influence others positively with their presence and can-do attitude that's contagious to everyone they come in contact. I also believe it's a quality that can be developed and enhanced. Many leaders possess this quality as well as people we perceive to be natural leaders. If you have strong executive presence, you and those around you, recognize it. It's the way you carry yourself, how you walk, talk and communicate. It's an uncanny ability to draw people into you and to make them want to listen to you, be with you and work for you.

There was a television commercial that used to come on that stated: "When E.F. Hutton talks, people listen." They would act out a scene of having people seated at a table in a restaurant and when E.F. Hutton would open his mouth at his small table the entire restaurant would become quiet to listen to whatever he had to say. I consider that an example of what having executive presence can do to others.

Many famous actors, CEOs, professional athletes, politicians have it and others recognize they have it without saying it. I believe many of us have experienced moments when things were going really well for us at work. I mean, we closed a big deal, completed a tough assignment or project, obtained a great performance rating and you're feeling extra special. It's these times when you feel invincible or as if you're walking on a cloud. When you're feeling like this and walk into a room for a meeting, you are more inclined to exemplify executive presence qualities.

The late Steve Jobs, President Barack Obama, Sir Richard Branson of the Virgin Group, and Oprah Winfrey are all considered to have executive presence. As you think of each of them what qualities come to mind? What are some of the common factors you would attribute to each of them? Steve Jobs is known to have been a great presenter. President Barack Obama is known to be a great communicator, Sir Richard Branson is a great entrepreneur and Oprah is known as a highly connected and influential personality. All of them look very different, have different backgrounds and experiences but all of them have great follower-ship, charisma, confidence and courage. They all are focused on making a positive impact and a difference in the lives of others.

Anthony Robbins states, "Success leaves clues." We can learn and develop our executive presence by observing and essentially applying and practicing the qualities that create great executive presence in others. I'd like us to begin by completing the following table on our understanding of how we are currently perceived by others. I'd like this to be a starting point to give us an indication of how we are currently perceived so we will be able to identify areas of opportunity to focus and prioritize.

This is similar to doing a self-analysis of a 360 assessment that provides leaders with an assessment of what others think of them in various categories depending on the focus of the assessment. I've implemented 360 assessments for many of my senior leader coaching clients that gave them insight and areas of opportunity for improvement primarily in leadership areas. The purpose is to allow them to gain insights in their blind spots to help them identify and change in areas that will make the biggest positive impact for them going forward. In most cases, based on their 360 assessments, I would work with them and their leaders on creating a development program and we would have the goal of completing another 360 assessment 6 to 12 months later to gauge the difference. I'd like us to use this template in a similar manner. This is a start, but it would be beneficial for you to get direct feedback from the others in the listed categories to provide you with their feedback so it's real and usable.

Fill in the blanks on the table below. Rate how you think your leader, co-workers, direct reports and others your work with (like your customers) perceive you on a scale of 1–10 (1 being the lowest rating and 10 being highest rating in the areas listed in the left column and first row).

	Leader	Co-workers	Direct Reports	Others
Presentation Skills				
Writing Skills/ Emails				
Listening & Interpersonal Skills				
Analytical Acumen & Critical Thinking				
Poise Under Pressure				
Charismatic/ Charm				
Authenticity				
Appearance				
Decisiveness				
Witty/Sense Of Humor				

RECOMMENDATIONS ON LEADERSHIP SKILLS THAT IMPACT EXECUTIVE PRESENCE

Presentation skills

I covered the impact of communication on presentation skills in Chapter 7 *Learn To Present As If Your Career Depends On It Because It Does.* This is one of the primary areas that demonstrates executive presence. This is a critical skill to develop and to make an area of focus for enhancing your presence. Please take action on the suggestions in that chapter and now apply it for the goal of improving your perceived executive presence.

Since executive presence has a lot to do with your confidence in various areas, becoming a great presenter is indeed a confidence booster. Getting to a place where you have a comfort in doing presentations to VIPs and being able to present when called on last minute illustrates your effectiveness. This is an area that's in your control. Decide to become a great presenter and gain a reputation as a "go-to person" when it comes to being able to articulate your ideas effectively and to connect with others in a personal manner.

I've heard one of the world's most recognized motivators, Les Brown, state:

> "Never make a point without a story and never tell a story without a point."

This is a great key to implement in the pursuit of leveraging presentation skills to enhance your executive presence. Storytelling is a great skill to possess in aiding in the development of your presentation skills. However, when presenting at work the stories should be relevant, concise and based on facts to support your statements or provide additional insight for others to better comprehend your point.

An example of this could be if I'm reviewing a PowerPoint presentation and have a point that states, "Effective storytelling can make a presentation more impactful." I could just read it and go on to the next bullet or give a specific example in the form of a story such as the following. I attended the town hall by the CEO and we had an opportunity for a Q&A session with him. I noticed whenever he would respond to a question he would answer it and provide an example of things that he does or is doing to address the problem. One question was related to how does he stay close to those on the front lines of the organization dealing with customers. He shared how he not only has town halls throughout the world but also intimate lunch meetings with just a dozen employees once a month. This setting allows them and the CEO to ask each other questions and gain insights into what's happening at all levels of the organization.

Think of telling stories as giving real world examples to help amplify a point. You don't have to do it on every point of discussion but it can go a long way to intersperse it throughout a presentation. The goal is to connect with your audience at a deeper level, to engage them during your presentations. Another area is your ability to orchestrate an interactive meeting. In some cases, meetings can get a little out of control if there are too many different people asking and answering questions when you're responsible for leading the meeting. It's important to be able to demonstrate you are effectively leading and directing things during a question and answer session. Especially when you have other subject matter experts in the room who have the answers that you don't.

This is called being a great facilitator. It's like being a quarterback of a football team. Knowing the plays but as the quarterback you get to lead the plays while at the same time know where everyone is on the field. It's up to you to leverage the strengths of each player at the right time to effectively execute a play. It's the same idea at work when leading an interactive meeting with others in the room. Sometimes you may throw a pass to a wide receiver that is open on the field but at the end of the play everyone returns to the line of scrimmage and you have the ball back in your hands. When leading a meeting and allowing others to respond, it's important that you facilitate the play by acknowledging the question and publicly stating you would like the subject matter expert (SME) to respond. After the SME responds immediately take the ball back in your hands by speaking up to move to the next point. Do your best to minimize a back and forth from the questioner and the person who asked the question. You can do this effectively by interjecting and doing a quick summary of the response and then transition. Being able to facilitate smoothly is another example that aids in your executive presence.

Writing Emails

Emails are the most popular way of communicating in the work environment today. Take a quick survey and look at how many emails you received on this past work week. Now try to determine how many emails you sent during this same period. Plus, if you add in your personal emails it can be a large number. Practically everyone at work is using it as his or her primary way of communicating but not everyone is doing it in a most effective manner. Most in corporate have been trained on how best to write in general, but scribing an email is different than drafting a traditional business memorandum.

In this section, I will keep the focus in the context of offering recommendations for email writing to improve your executive presence. Since writing emails is so widely used, it's a great opportunity to distinguish you from others and improve your image. My approach in this area is similar to my approach around effective oral presentations. I like to take into account the impact of communication based on how you look and sound and a smaller amount on the content. How many emails do you receive and open, but after first glance you decide not to read it in its entirety? Think about the reasons why you choose not to read some emails in full versus others. For this exercise, let's take out the factor of whom it's coming from because I understand that you might be more inclined to read an entire email from your leader than from someone else. Let's assume the email is coming from the same person with the same subject line and urgency level. My hypothesis is depending on how it "looks" to you will determine if you choose to read it all at that moment, glance through it for any action items for you or to speed read to get a high level overview of the context. I'm sure there are some people in your organization that have a reputation of writing emails that you prefer not to read based primarily on how it comes across at first glance. The old saying that the first 30 seconds of a meeting makes the difference also applies to emails.

What I'm highlighting is all related to the look and readability of an email. This is the part of email writing and reading I want to focus this section on. Let's begin by evaluating how you organize your emails from the subject line to who is in the "to" box versus the "cc" box. How do you begin your emails? How is the information organized and presented? How do you conclude?

As an exercise and way to assess how you currently write your emails, please go to your sent folder and look up recent work email to a group of people. Beyond the content, if you received this email what is the likelihood that you would want to read it—on a scale of 1–10 and 10 being most likely to read it and 1 being you would delete it at first glance? How organized is it written? Is there a clear introduction, body and conclusion? Is it an email to request action or is it information only and can you easily understand it from the email? Is your email all words with multiple paragraphs or do you use bullets, numbers, indentations, pictures or tables?

All of these questions are related to factors that help increase the readability of your email. Simultaneously, it also impacts your executive presence. The better the readability, the better your image relating to writing effective emails.

The following is an example of the same email presented it two different ways to help illustrate the point.

Example 1

To: Everyone on the team
Cc: All of our leaders

Subject: Meeting Recap

Hi everyone,

I hope this email finds all of you well and that you are having a great day.

Justin from Finance, Jenay in Legal, Amen in Marketing, Joy in Advertising and my colleague Windy and I met with the C-levels and their representatives at our largest client X. We shared with them our proposal to not only retain the business we have but also to expand it. We presented several of our new product solutions that would help them reduce their costs and become more efficient. At the end of our presentation, we discussed our financial offer for a 5-year agreement that will allow us to retain our business and will minimize the probability of them considering an RFP.

The C-level contacts at the customer included Daren the CEO, Thom the COO, Chris the CTO, Kelley and Anindya from Human Resources. They all attended and had the following people from their respective teams; Jessie, Norman, Banks, G.G., Darlene, Ray, Anthony, Frank, Denise, Thomas, Nikki, Star and Nakayo. They had several questions to better understand our new product solutions and our marketing plan. However, the majority of our time was spent answering questions about our financial offer and the 5-year agreement. We negotiated on the spot and will be making some concessions in our financial proposal in order to get them their commitment for a 5 year-agreement. The concessions will minimize our profitability with this client but we are considering this a lost leader since this client is the largest and has the highest market share in their industry. We can leverage this partnership to help us acquire other large customers and expand our share. We also included parameters in our agreement to be able to have them be a reference for us in our acquisition and retention strategies with other organizations we are targeting and who will be up for renewal in the next few years.

They are planning to have a follow-up internal discussion and will let us know their final decision. We gave them a 1-week timeline to respond to us or our offer will expire and they agreed. We also had them sign an NDA. We also included details that include financial penalties if they decide not to proceed with us. However, we are optimistic they will sign the agreement so we can have a fruitful strategic relationship over the next 5 years.

Have a great day and thank you!

Jeff

Example 2

To: Windy, Jenay, Amen, Justin, Joy (Only those who need to know or need to take action and in order of their level)

Cc: Only those who need to be aware of this meeting because they will or have some impact to this client

Subject: Client X Meeting Recap & Next Steps

Hi everyone,

My team and I met with Client X to present our proposal to retain and expand our business for 5 years and the following is a high level recap and next steps.

Meeting Recap:

- Met with C levels and their representatives as they are all very interested in our partnership

- They liked our marketing presentation and expressed an interest in our new product solutions

- We negotiated the parameters of our financial offer and came to a consensus

Next Steps and Action Items:

- They will respond by next week with either a signed contract or a decision not to proceed

- Justin and Jenay, please reach out to your contacts to ensure we are in alignment on the agreement and that they understand the financial benefits for them

- Windy and I will reach out to our contacts tomorrow to answer questions and reinforce our value proposition

I will provide another update next week

Thank you,

Jeff

Notice the difference? The first example is written to everyone and copying everyone else. It has wording and information that's not necessary. At first glance it looks like several paragraphs that are not appealing to read.

The second one is much more concise and written to only those who need to know or take action. Those copied are people who need to be in the know because they have something to do with this client.

The idea is to present your ideas in writing in such a way to make it simple and easy to read and understand the what, why, who, when, where and how.

Listening and Interpersonal Skills

Zig Ziglar has a quote that says "People don't care how much you know until they know how much you care … about them." The more impactful you are with your ability to demonstrate your interest in others by effective listening and engagement the more likely it is for you to demonstrate executive presence. Focusing on what's important to others goes a long way in others looking up to you as a genuine leader.

Listening goes beyond using your two ears but should engage all of your senses. The goal should be to sincerely be interested in others as they speak. Those with executive presence learn how to tune out others and to give their full attention to the person speaking in front of them. I observed senior level leaders at American Express do this so well that at a Global Sales meeting with over 1,000 people in attendance. Each person I spoke with about the senior leader would state how impressed they were with him. He had a gift for making everyone feel appreciated because of his ability to give him or her his full attention even though they only had a few moments to share with him.

I met and had a chance to speak with Ken Chenault, the CEO of American Express, before and after a town hall session. I felt I got to know him personally because he gave me an opportunity to speak with him and he primarily just listened to what I had to say. It made me feel heard which made me like him even more.

I suggest we do the same when dealing with others at work. I recognize that there are poor examples of senior leaders who will share they are good at multi tasking. I recall another senior leader who would have meetings in his office and my VP and I had an opportunity to share and get his input on what we considered to be a very important initiative. When it was time for our meeting, we could see he was working on his computer and speaking on the phone so we tapped on his door to alert him of our presence. When he turned to see us, he waved us to enter. After he completed his call he turned away from us to face his computer and he began what appeared to be responding to emails and asked us to begin. We began our important presentation while this senior level leader was not looking at us or facing us but was responding to emails. He shared that he liked multi-tasking to save time and he learned to be effective at doing two things at the same time. We presented our presentation and he paused and asked a few questions.

I don't know how effective it was for him to respond to emails and listen to our presentation at the same time. However, I do know how it made us feel. We felt underappreciated, disrespected and that what we had to share was not important to him. I share this story as an example of the opposite of the potential impact of not fully listening with all of your senses. Do you want to have executive presence? Listening to others is a major key. It helps others feel you care which in turn causes them to care about what's important to you.

Analytical Acumen/Critical Thinking

Analytic acumen is your ability to not only understand numbers but also having a demonstrated capacity to analyze information and the ability to take action on it. Regardless of your position in corporate, if you are an individual contributor in an entry-level role or if you're a leader in middle management, it's important that you learn to analyze data.

The higher the level, the more critical it tends to be that the skills on the senior levels are consistently helping them assess their business. It helps you to make more effective decisions that are based on reviewing trends to help you forecast possible outcomes.

In January 2014, the American Management Association completed a study regarding Analytical Acumen and Critical thinking that I want to share. Nearly one in five millennials (19%) are perceived to be lacking analytical skills when compared with other generations in the workplace, according to a study sponsored by American Management Association (AMA).

The survey looked at how prepared organizations are to compete in an age of Big Data and involved nearly 800 respondents from more than 50 industries. Participants were asked to assess the analytical skills of their employees by age group. With a combined 58% rated as advanced or expert, the Gen X cohort's analytical strength was rated highest, followed by Baby Boomers with 41% and Millennials with 35%. "Despite their familiarity with technology, Millennials aren't seen as being equally analytics savvy," said AMA Senior Vice President Robert G. Smith. "But what's really at issue here is an analytical mindset, which includes both quantitative and qualitative ability more than any specific number-crunching skill. In other words, employees need to know what to look for, what questions to ask, and how to make inferences and draw conclusions based on data in order to drive the organization forward."

Regardless of what generational bucket you fall into, know that analytical acumen and critical thinking are major to being perceived as having executive presence. If you don't feel like you're analytical, I strongly encourage you to add it to your development plan and search out your peers or others who have this important skill as it will benefit you long term as you continue to expand and make the most of your current and future roles.

Poise Under Pressure

Most corporate environments are dynamic and fast paced with big goals and expectations. Pressure is the norm. Poise is being controlled, balanced and even tempered regardless of the situation. Not that you're not feeling the pressure but you don't appear to be as affected by the pressure. It's not panicking or losing your calm when getting bad news about something not going the way you thought. How do you handle situations when you're caught off guard? When something unexpected happens that's not good for you or your team or organization, how do you handle it? The way you respond is a reflection on your executive presence.

The biggest suggestion for maintaining your composure under pressure is to remember that things will happen and will come up at the most inopportune times. The more we remember that this is part of the corporate environment, the better we can deal with the situation and stay calm to make the best decision on how to handle and resolve it. We are able to think more effectively when we are in control of our emotions. It's fine to acknowledge your feelings but recognize where you're at in a given moment and recall that you have the choice to either react or respond.

Many boxers like to antagonize their opponents as a strategy to get them off their game. Muhammad Ali was known to intentionally use this strategy in an effort to cause his opponent to lose their cool and to forget their strategy and approach and wildly try to beat up Ali. That's the moment Ali would take advantage; by having them tire out or swing wildly because they were not in a controlled state. Ali, being in a controlled position would use this approach to outsmart his opponents and win a match that he may not have won had his opposition stayed poised under pressure. There are many movies where they show people panicking under pressure and pay a dear price because of it, versus others who remain calm and think through an approach that can save their life. Think about some of the movies where the audience is hollering, "Don't open that door!"

As a leader and as an individual you are always under the microscope. Others are watching how we act in the various situations that come up at work. Anyone can respond positively to good news. However, people with the characteristic of having poise under pressure are perceived more positively and as having executive presence.

Charisma/Fascinating

Charisma is defined as a compelling attractiveness or charm that can inspire devotion in others. You know it when you see it. When they walk in a room people seem to be drawn to them. People with this quality know how to work a room and make everyone they meet with feel special. They have the ability to uplift the spirit of a person and even a room. The interesting thing is if you have this quality, others see it in you and you do not have to tell anyone you have it. They would know it. There is sometimes a buzz in the air about this person that most people recognize and like. They are very much people oriented and they connect well to others.

In Sally Hogshead's book titled *Fascinate—Your 7 Triggers to Persuasion and Captivation,* she writes: "Fascination has little to do with what you say and everything to do with what you inspire others to say about your message." In addition, "The true measure of fascination lives not in your own communication to the world, but in how the world communicates about you."

In order to enhance your charisma and become more fascinating in an effort to improve your executive presence, work on enhancing your self-esteem. The better we think and feel about ourselves in a positive and non-conceited manner, the more likely we are to draw others to us. It allows us to feel good about ourselves and that's what becomes like a magnet. People are naturally attracted to others who are happy, upbeat, optimistic and self-confident. It has less to do with physical appearance and more to do with intrinsic qualities.

Authenticity

Since I wrote on Authentic Leadership in Chapter 6, I'll just highlight a few areas for you to consider relating authenticity to executive presence. Consider authenticity from the perspective of how others view you being genuine. All of the qualities I'm highlighting are interconnected. All of them impact how you are perceived. A good way to improve your image in this category is by being transparent. Be willing to share your highs, lows, mistakes and lessons learned.

Sharing the good, bad and ugly about yourself, humbles you and causes others to be able to better relate to you. Being relatable, sincere and open to share demonstrates your confidence in yourself and shows you care about helping other's which illustrates authenticity.

Some are more comfortable than others in being transparent about themselves. However, I encourage you to work on opening up more and sharing. Begin sharing a little and see how people respond and how it causes them to view you as an authentic leader.

The more genuine we can be, the more it attracts others to us. I recognize that many try to pretend they are someone they're not and they don't realize how it tends to cause them to be viewed as disingenuous. People love the real us. We are beautifully unique, special and different. We all have a unique fingerprint for a reason. We all have different experiences, gifts and talents. We are each a unique person the world has never seen before and it's purposeful. It allows us to bring things to the work environment that only we can.

Being the real deal is being authentic which demonstrates to others that you have executive presence. It's a confidence builder to be comfortable in your own skin, knowing and believing that you are special. Walk in your greatness and of being authentically you knowing being you is enough. Just make sure you are authentically being your best you.

Appearance

I recognize that appearance is a major aspect of executive presence. However, I was hesitant to include a section in this book on appearance because this can be a sensitive subject. It can be sensitive more so today than in the past because the corporate environment has changed in this area and varies per industry and geography. I currently live in Northern California near Silicon Valley where it's known to be a casual dress environment. However, Financial Services companies in New York expect suit and ties or suits without a tie. Appearance today in corporate is more sensitive to other factors such as diversity and that people have a right to express themselves as long as they are getting their work done or that's at least the prevailing sentiment.

My question to you is does your appearance affect your success at work? As you ponder this question here are a few other things to bear in mind.

Terri Savelle Foy who is an author and success coach states, "What you wear may not define your value as a person, but it does reflect how you feel about yourself and your attitude towards life." I think this is a powerful statement worth thinking about. Since I get to work from home most of the time, I can easily get comfortable wearing sweats and dressing very casually. However, I notice on the days when I have meetings, I dress in a suit for in-person meetings. When the meeting ends early and I come home dressed and continue working in a suit, it does tend to make me feel better about myself. What are your observations in this regard?

Another consideration regarding the impact of our appearance at work related to our executive presence is the statement that people make judgments based on the first 30 seconds of what they see. The American Personnel Consultants state that hiring leaders make a decision to hire or not in the first 30 seconds of meeting someone. They also state your clothing is responsible for 95% of that first impression. Bearing in mind that this is before they get to know you or allow you time to share your accomplishments.

Based on an article by Clothes Psychology your clothing tells others about who you are and who you want to be. The article states there are a variety of types of dressers:

• **The Sloppy Dresser:** When you do not look together, your clothes are wrinkled, stained or just don't match. It tells the people around you that you're sloppy too. You don't put in the effort to make sure that your appearance is decent.

• **The Designer Dresser:** When you're always sporting a designer pair of shoes, or you are seen with three different types of designer purses people may view you not only as successful and together but materialistic as well.

• **The Skimpy Dresser:** These people are looking for the attention. Women that wear the tight clothing, revealing cleavage and other body parts want a sense of power, which sends the message that they are insecure and need that attention in order to validate themselves.

The Business Casual Dresser: This individual shows off a certain confidence especially in the work field and earns the respect of their co-workers.

The Flashy Dresser: These people like to be noticed! They want others to see their fun side and they try to show it with their accessories. Maybe they'll wear red lipstick with an all black outfit, or they'll put on a pair of bright orange jeans, either way these people get noticed for their flashy style, and the fact that they're trend setters not followers.

The Drab Dresser: These people unlike the flashy dresser don't necessarily want to be noticed. They typically dress in neutrals and try to blend in with the crowd being trend followers not setters.

The Athletic Dresser: These dressers have to be extra careful not to be perceived as sloppy. They are very active and love to wear work out clothes as a part of their daily wardrobe.

The Goth Dresser: These individuals typically favor one color, black. Therefore they can come across as unapproachable or depressed.

The Casual Dresser: You could be the most creative person out there but if you dress in the same style every day and never put any personality or flair into your outfits you can come across as just the opposite ... boring.

I'm sharing this information as data for you to consider how you are currently perceived based on your dress at work. If your goal is to improve your executive presence what will you do differently based on the information provided? It should depend on your values and what you desire to get out of your current situation. Bear in mind that if you want something different you have to do something different.

Decisiveness

Decisiveness is the ability to make a choice quickly and confidently. This is an important trait to have in the fast and high paced corporate environments. It's a good quality to have but it's not as simple as it might seem. As a leader or individual contributor, it's important that the decisions you make are thought out and based on solid business reasons. It's also helpful to get input from others and leverage your previous relevant experiences before making the call. It can be a risky and high impact decision. If you pull the trigger with the goal of being considered decisive and it's the wrong decision, it could cost you your job. It's very important that you do your best to get it right. However, there's a balance in making effective decisions in a timely manner because if you get caught up in analysis paralysis and attempt to get input from many others, it could cause you to miss out on what could have been a great opportunity.

The "Ladder of Inference" was developed by organizational psychologist Chris Argyris and used by Peter Senge in *The Fifth Discipline: The Art and Practice of the Learning Organization.* It's a ladder that outlines the process of how people draw conclusions to take action. I'm referencing it as it relates to the process we may go through to make decisions at work.

At the bottom of the ladder are reality and facts. We apply our assumptions regardless if they are recognized or not and we draw conclusions or make decisions based on the interpreted facts and our assumptions. We develop beliefs based on these conclusions. We take action that seems right to us since they are based on what we believe.

The idea of using the ladder of inference to help us make more effective decisions is to question our current assumptions. To recognize how we naturally make decisions and to be willing to challenge it by questioning and testing our assumptions and being willing to challenge it by obtaining external input.

Another point of consideration is how we feel after making a decision. People start to question if they made the right choice. The renowned American psychologist Leon Festinger defined cognitive dissonance as the discomfort people experience when they hold two conflicting ideas or beliefs. He found that because it is uncomfortable to hold two conflicting beliefs, people reduce their dissonance by focusing their attention on only the data that supports their decision, and they avoid and ignore the data that doesn't support their belief. The process creates dogmatism because people want to defend the decision they've already made.

As we go down the path of being more decisive to improve our executive presence, let's be sure to check our decision making process. Be willing to adjust as necessary to improve our probability of getting it right the first time.

Sense of Humor

Having a sense of humor can go a long way in the challenging and fast paced corporate environment. Having the talent to recognize a tense situation and being able to lighten up a room by a timely comment that is relevant to the audience can make a big difference. This is a trait that goes with those with executive presence. They tend to be witty and have a gift of being able to inject comedy to help a situation or to make a point more acceptable by others.

It's not trying to be a comedian or a class clown of sorts. Nor is it always going around telling jokes and slapping people on their back at the punch line. It's more of being witty, in the moment and spontaneous. It's using humor as a tool in part of your ability to communicate a message or help others digest a message. It's the ability to know when and when not to use humor based on your audience and their ability to receive it.

This type of humor can be developed. The primary way is by observing others who use it effectively. This is one of the ways I learned to develop my sense of humor. I had leaders in a variety of companies who I reported to that were really good at using humor at the right times during internal meetings and when we would be with clients. By observing them, it let me know that it was acceptable for me to do. Your corporate culture will let you know what's acceptable in this regard.

Since I was able to see other leaders use their humor, it gave me the permission to do the same. I'd imagine most of you reading this have a natural sense of humor when you're with family and friends. Feeling that you are in a safe environment, you are more than likely able to perceive an opportunity to make a humorous comment and you go for it. It's the same concept at work. When you feel comfortable and when you can be yourself at work, it's a matter of being willing to test the waters. Initially, you may bomb but that's okay and it's part of the process. The more you do it, the better you get at it.

I reported to a VP in a past role who instituted a rule that if you were late to a team call you better be prepared to share a funny story or tell a joke. This allowed everyone a lot of practice and it also taught the team how to find appropriate work humor.

Adding humor to your personal branding package will go a long way in allowing you to be more liked and enhance your executive presence.

I would like to challenge you to review this section and measure your results on the assessment. Work on the areas of opportunity as it is all about your personal brand. There are many books that outline the importance of viewing yourself as You Inc. It's up to you to do your part in marketing yourself by your image and reputation which are all within your control. I ask that you put the odds in your favor in helping to better distinguish yourself from the crowd and consistently demonstrate your executive presence.

CHAPTER 9

Networking

"The richest people in the world look for and build networks; everyone else looks for work." —ROBERT KIYOSAKI

MY CORPORATE BACKGROUND is primarily working in sales and sales leadership roles. An aspect of sales is account management that focuses on managing, retaining and expanding customer relationships. Organizations place a lot of resources towards these initiatives such as special financial arrangements, senior leadership attention, technology support, the best customer service, invitations to events, lunches, dinners, etc. and an assigned sales person. The level depends on the nature of the business relationship. Some customer relationships are more strategic than others. The larger the business relationship and market share with the client is a determining factor of how much service and attention they are provided.

Out of all the resources invested in clients the most impactful one is the relationship manager. The relationship manager can have various titles but the essence of their role is to be the company's ambassador with the client. Depending on the industry and what they are providing to the customer, they would want to have full account penetration. The idea is to get to know as many people in the most senior-levels of their client organization.

One sales position I held was working with clients who had annual revenue over $2B and I was essentially selling automated payment solutions. In order to get my solution implemented in their organization, I needed to work with their CFO, Treasurer, CPO, CTO and others reporting up through these senior level contacts. In some cases, I may start with the person over Accounts Payable and would need to build a strong relationship with them to be introduced to their Treasurer and CFO. Simultaneously, I would need to connect with their technology team, as the solution needed their buy-in as well. Essentially, the larger the client and opportunity, the longer the sales cycle. In addition, the bigger the sales opportunity, the more a company is willing to invest in making the expansion happen.

The foundation of it happening is the relationship that the account manager establishes with the client. The more the account managers know about the business the better. In addition, the best account managers also build a personal relationship with all the contacts and should be able to tell you as much as possible about them personally as well as the business.

Harvey MacKay, the author of *Swim With the Sharks Without Being Eatin' Alive,* is known for having all of his sales people complete a 66-question profile. MacKay's 66-question profile states "It's critical to have information about your customer." Armed with the right knowledge, we can outsell, out manage, out motivate and out negotiate our competitors. Knowing your customer means knowing what your customer really wants. Maybe it's your product, but maybe there is something else too— recognition, respect, reliability, service, friendship and help. Things all of us care more about as human beings than we care about products or services. Once you attach your personality to the proposition, people start reacting to the personality, and stop reacting to the proposition."

The profile has questions for the account manager to answer in the following categories about their customer: Education, family, business background, special interests, lifestyle and your knowledge from working with the client. The better job the account manager does by demonstrating value to build a strong relationship, the better the business relationship can be. When it's done well, the account manager will be able to retain, grow and benefit from the relationship. I use this as the background to explain the significance of networking to build strong personal and business relationships.

In his book *Click—Ten Truths for Building Extraordinary Relationships,* George Fraser points out to tailor your relationships. He says to consciously create the perfect fit. He also says to nurture your relationships for they are the core of personal and professional success. This is based on the golden rule of do unto others, as you would have them do to you. I also like what is referred to as the Platinum rule by Tony Alessandra, "Treat others the way they want to be treated." This aligns with Stephen Covey's Habit 5 of "Seek first to understand, then to be understood." Zig Ziglar's popular quote of "You can have everything in life you want if you will just help enough other people get what they want."

All these points help to describe that the major aspects of building relationships should be about helping others. The more we take the focus off of ourselves and our needs and explore supporting others first, it will naturally cause others to be willing to support our efforts. It's like farming, sowing good seed and cultivating it. Over time, they will reap a harvest based on the type of seed planted. If you plant orange seeds and cultivate it properly, over time you will receive an orange tree with many oranges and more seeds. It's interesting how what we do can have exponential returns.

An example of applying this same concept to networking and building relationships is how I helped someone who lost his job. I provided him with coaching. After he obtained a job and built a positive reputation in his organization, he referred me to his boss' boss who was looking for an executive coach. Having coached the person who was the CTO, he introduced me to their head of sales and their CFO and CEO. This turned into a 3-year leadership development contract and coaching of their executive management team and all of their people leaders.

Think about it. It all began from "sowing a seed" to help someone else through a tough time.

I had a previous relationship with the person and when I heard he lost his job I offered to provide him with coaching services in exchange for him to help me create a video for my website. He had a previous background in creating professional music videos. My thought with coaching is there has to be some type of investment to demonstrate commitment by the person being coached. I learned that when people get things of value without any investment they tend not to esteem it as highly. The old saying of "no investment, no return" applies. Instead of offering the coaching without any investment, I was able to help my friend get a sense of obligation to apply the coaching I was providing him. As a result, it helped him to rebuild his confidence and obtain a new job.

SYNERGISTIC RELATIONSHIPS

Synergistic relationships are based on two or more people or entities working together to form an enhanced outcome for all involved. This is what networking should produce when all involved are willing to put the necessary time and effort into the relationship so everyone benefits beyond what they would have without working together. The key is for both parties to be willing to commit to the relationship.

I mentioned cultivating a seed that's been planted and the same concept applies to professional relationships. Cultivation is defined by Merriam Webster dictionary as to prepare and use (soil) for growing plants, to grow and care for (plants), to grow or raise (something) under conditions that you can control. It's about making the effort to build the relationship so that it grows. The way we cultivate a seed is by tending to the ground, pulling weeds, keeping the rodents and birds away; ensuring that the ground is watered sufficiently and receives sunlight. It's creating ideal conditions for the seed to grow. Examples of this in networking would be after you have met someone you had an organic connection with. You may want to send an email, make a phone call, or even schedule a meeting over coffee to get better acquainted and explore specific areas of interest for both of you. It's important to have a goal in mind that you are working towards, as it will allow for a more mutually beneficial relationship.

SIX DEGREES OF SEPARATION

The concept of "six degrees of separation" is based on the premise that any two people are six or fewer links apart. In other words, you know someone who knows someone who knows someone who knows someone who knows someone who knows the president or anyone else for that matter. There is also a game based on the concept called "Six degrees of Kevin Bacon." I bring this to your attention to remind you that if you leverage your relationships effectively and cultivate them you can be connected with the person who has your dream job. It's about cultivating and building our relationships so we are not calling them when we are in desperate need. I'm sure you can appreciate when people reach out to you who you do not know but they want you to help them get a job.

Take a moment to think about some of the people you personally know who you think are highly connected and influential. I'm sure we all have them when we take a moment to think about it. I'm not referring to people we are connected to on social media. I'm referring to people where you are on a first name basis. I knew someone who knew the president of a division at a company where I was interviewing and I reached out to him. He was happy to accommodate and provided me with a reference that helped me to land the job.

Many of us forget the power of networking or we are hesitant to ask for help from our contacts. The more we are open to helping others and connecting people we know to help them, the more inclined we will be to do the same. I get a lot of people reaching out to me to make connections. If I personally know them, I will do whatever I can. If I don't know them directly, I'm still willing to accommodate but they will need to set everything up for me to make the connection easier. In other words, if they notice I'm connected to someone in my network that works for Google and they have an upcoming interview. I'd like them to inform me of the department, the position and the person they are interviewing with so it will be easy for me to just pass along this information to my direct contact. However, if they are vague and do not have an interview and just want to speak to my contact, I may hesitate. My thought is everyone is very busy and his or her time is valuable. Most don't mind helping but they don't want to feel like they are doing all the heavy lifting on behalf of someone they don't even know directly.

Networking should be value based for both parties. When you're requesting something from someone else, look for ways that you can demonstrate value to him or her. Make your requests very specific and do all that you can to minimize effort and time on their end. This approach will get you more responses.

IMPACT OF RELATIONSHIPS

Jim Rohn, the late motivational speaker said, "You are the average of the five people you spend the most time with." Take a moment and reflect on that statement. Think about your five closest friends and their financial state, their home, career, family life, etc. Does this statement ring true for you? Dennis Kimbro the author of *The Wealth Choice* stated: "If you are the smartest person in your group, you need a new group." Our closest relationships have the biggest impact on our lives just as our environment does. Since we spend the most time with our closest five friends we tend to think alike, have similar beliefs and live in comparable neighborhoods. Dennis Kimbro's point relates to the definition of insanity that states, "If you keep doing the same things over and over and expecting different results, you're insane." If we want to expand our thinking and way of life to get more, we should put ourselves in an environment with people who are living what we aspire to be, do and have. Not at the detriment of our current friends but to help raise the stakes for ourselves which can also positively impact our friends.

The idea of not being the smartest in your group relates to sports as well. I took up golf years ago prior to having children and paid for professional lessons. As I continued to spend time at the range practicing, playing on weekends and taking lessons, my game improved, but I would only occasionally break the score of 100. My golf professional informed me that I needed to play with players who were better than me in order to take my golf game to another level and consistently score below 100. I began playing with others from work who were members of country clubs and very good which ultimately helped me improve my game and reach my goal. I learned a lot playing with the better players and even before they offered suggestions to help me improve my game, it naturally improved from me simply being in the company of better players.

In his bestselling book *The Tipping Point,* Malcolm Gladwell cites a classic 1974 study by sociologist Mark Granovetter that surveyed how a group of men in Newton, Massachusetts, found their current job. The study was titled "Getting a Job." Granovetter discovered that 56% of those surveyed found their current job through a personal connection. Only 19% used what was considered traditional job searching routes at the time such as job listings and executive recruiters. Roughly 10% applied directly to an employer and obtained the job.

Personal contacts are a key to opening doors. However, that's not a surprise. What is surprising, however, is that of those personal connections that reaped dividends for those in the study, only 17% saw their personal contact often. As much as they would if they were good friends. 55% saw their contact only occasionally and 28% barely met with their contact at all. In other words, it's not necessarily strong contacts, like family and close friends that prove the most powerful. Often, the most impactful people in our network are those who are acquaintances.

As a result of the study, Granovetter coined the phrase "The strength of weak ties" by showing that when it comes to finding out about new jobs or new information or new ideas "weak ties" are generally more important than those you consider strong. Many of your closest friends and contacts go to the same outings, generally do the same work, and exist in roughly the same world as you do. That's why they seldom know information that you don't already know. Your weak ties, on the other hand, generally occupy a very different world than you do. They're hanging out with different people, often in different worlds, with access to a whole inventory of knowledge and information unavailable to you and your close friends.

This illustrates the importance of networking beyond your closest friends and exposing yourself to other groups, organizations and settings. Your long term goals should influence your networking choices so you're not all over the place and scattered doing everything to network with as many people as possible. Networking should be strategic, purposeful and value driven. If you're interested in obtaining a position in the marketing group of your current organization and you're in sales, you should intentionally network with other marketing contacts in your organization and outside your company. Great considerations for strategic networking opportunities should include Employee resource groups, non-profit/community organizations and cross-functional teams.

EMPLOYEE RESOURCE GROUPS (ERGS)

Employee resource groups are internal company groups of people who have something in common with a stated focus. They normally are made up of a group of internal professionals representing various levels and functional areas of a company. They are also known as affinity groups or business network groups.

Diversity Best Practices 2011 benchmarking and assessment outlined the top employee resource groups of U.S. based companies:

1. Women
2. Lesbian, Gay, Bisexual and Transgender Employees
3. Multicultural men and women (i.e., African Americans, Asians, Hispanics, etc.)
4. Military Veterans
5. People with Disabilities
6. Generational Groups
7. Working Parents
8. Religious Groups
9. Single Parents

When I worked in New York for American Express and when I worked for Wells Fargo in San Francisco, I was a member of their Black Employee Networks. We had professional development sessions, networking opportunities with social functions and senior level leader speakers. It was great for me, especially when I was a new employee in a new city. It allowed me to make connections and build friendships that helped out long term. It also allowed me to build relationships with senior level leaders who later helped me in getting a promotion and a position as well.

One of the main ideas of ERGs is to allow people who have something in common to come together in a corporate environment. Many companies have an annual employee survey to gauge the engagement of their employees. ERGs are a great way for them to allow employees to connect with other employees in the same organization to learn and share with each other. I wrote in an earlier chapter how the Gallup organization provides many of the employee surveys in corporate. One of the questions they normally include is *"Do you have a best friend at work?"* One of the reasons is this question helps to determine how connected the employee is internally in their organization. Employees with more connections in the company are more likely to stay engaged and employed with the company longer than someone who is not as connected. Employee resource groups provide a venue for people with commonality to build strong interpersonal relationships with networking that will ultimately help the individuals and the company.

When I began my speaking business, I would speak at all types of companies and a variety of employee resource groups.

I spoke to ERGs focused on ethnicity, nationality, gender, religious affiliations and others. The common thread among them all was their connection to a common theme inside an organization. This provided a platform for them to share their challenges and to offer their experiences and talents in a non-threatening environment. It's all voluntary so I would see lower level employees taking on bigger responsibilities than their normal job function and I would notice higher level leaders would gladly participate as well. This allowed all of them to work together towards a common goal without taking their titles into consideration of who would play what role in the group. In some cases, the ERG would have a senior level sponsor but was not involved in the regular meetings yet provided guidance and corporate endorsements when needed.

OTHER NETWORKING AREAS OF CONSIDERATION

There are many other avenues of establishing channels for mutually beneficial networking opportunities through community and non-profit organizations. I'll highlight two that have positively impacted my career:

1. Toastmasters International — I highlighted in an earlier chapter the benefits of Toastmasters and how it helped my career and my ability to present more effectively. As a reminder, Toastmasters International is a nonprofit educational organization that operates clubs worldwide for the purpose of helping members improve their communication, public speaking, and leadership skills. Another area where it benefited me long-term was the networking opportunities it provided. Toastmasters' clubs can be totally external to a company and in many cases they also have clubs in companies. Both are good but my primary experience with Toastmasters' organizations were outside of my company.

I've lived in several different cities where I was a member of a Toastmasters club. The first was in South Florida where I recall the majority of the members were retired professionals. I gained a lot of wisdom from attending the club in leadership and in dealing with various personalities of seniors. However, some of the members were business owners, attorneys and business executives. I was invited to homes and events from some of the members that gave me exposure to other powerful people I would not have met otherwise. The second club I joined was in Cincinnati, Ohio. It was in an office building with various tenants from all types of companies. This allowed me to build relationships in a city that I made deeper connections in and led me to helping others find jobs. I planted good seeds by helping others. Finally, I was a member and president of a club in New Jersey. This gave me an opportunity to meet other regional leaders at Toastmasters and attend bigger conferences that connected me with professional speakers. It gave me a sneak peek into what I'm doing today.

I strongly recommend joining Toastmasters as an opportunity to not only build your leadership and communication skills but also network and meet other noteworthy professionals.

2. **Religious Organizations like Churches** — Churches and the like can be great organizations to also build your leadership skills. This allows you to network and build life long relationships. I know many might go to church for the purpose of networking because they heard some very important people are members of a certain church. However, networking works better when the purpose is to give to others and establish mutually beneficial relationships. It should not be one sided for any particular person. The reason being, once you connect with the person and get what you want then will you go? Ideally, you would attend church to meet your spiritual needs and as a benefit you get to build relationships with others.

I highlight churches as many may attend religious institutions, but may not take advantage of all the church offers. Many of which would open up doors of opportunity for networking. Such as new members classes, community events and Bible studies since they tend to be in a more intimate environment than the typical Sunday congregation.

I joined my church, World Conquerors Church in Oakland, California, and immediately got involved with the men's meetings. This allowed me to get to know the other men in the church and many of their families on a personal basis. It helped me to build personal relationships naturally without wanting anything from them but friendship. Over the course of time, I started my coaching, training and speaking business and many of the men volunteered to help. One helped me set up my website, created my logo, brochures and business cards. Another helped with creating videos for my site and someone else did all of the editing and manuals for my clients. Other members of the church recommended me to their various companies that opened up doors for many of my business clients.

I included church as a networking opportunity because for me personally it has had the biggest impact in my life. I thought it was interesting that there were other churches I considered joining because some prospects attended but I decided to follow my convictions to join where I felt I needed to be in order to grow spiritually and everything else fell into place. I was not pursuing people, but allowed natural relationships to be established and those have been mutually beneficial.

Cross-Functional Teams

Participation in a cross-functional team is a great opportunity to make new connections and gain different experiences. Requests to work on cross-functional teams however typically happen when you're loaded with regular job responsibilities. Some don't initially view it as an opportunity but rather as added work and they just don't have the time. Most leaders ask those who are busy and getting things done to support an initiative where they would like input. In some cases they ask for volunteers but it's more likely to come as being "volun-told." If you embrace it, the end result is normally a fulfilling experience with new insights and connections that can be leveraged for future opportunities.

I consider this an area of opportunity to network and connect with others. I point this out as sometimes we may not initially view a new opportunity of working with others as a networking opportunity and some may pass on something that could help open major doors down the road. Throughout my career, I've had the opportunity to participate on cross-functional teams that have increased my knowledge about the business and other functional areas but also connected me with others who have helped to positively impact my career because I responded yes to the opportunity.

There's a movie that Jim Carrey starred in 2008 called *Yes Man*. Jim Carrey's character was stuck in a rut and was known by his friends and coworkers to be someone who constantly said no to almost any request. He later attends a motivational seminar and has to say yes to everything. As a result of saying "yes," he got a job promotion, new friends, more excitement and the woman of his dreams. All from saying *yes!*

I'm not suggesting you say yes to every request that comes your way, but I am stating you should strongly consider saying yes more often than not. (Remembering the points from Chapter 2 on *Time is Ticking*). It's amazing how many times we say yes to doing something related to working with others that turns into so much more than we originally thought. You know when the leader asks for a volunteer sometimes they want you to say yes so they don't have to plead to find someone. Next time your leader presents an opportunity to participate on a cross-functional team, make it easy on them and yourself by simply saying *yes!*

Associations

Other groups that I recommend you consider for networking opportunities are associations that can include university alumni, fraternities, sororities, MBA and Trade Associations, etc. Joining and actively participating in associations is an opportunity to build relationships naturally with others who have something in common with you.

After obtaining my MBA, I joined the National Black MBA Association and would attend their national conferences. Then national conferences included leadership development opportunities, motivational speakers (right up my alley), career fairs and other professional development and networking opportunities. I started out as a member who just attended to benefit from all of their offerings until a mentor informed me about the benefits of getting involved in my local chapter to maximize the benefits as well as share my expertise by volunteering to serve.

I began serving by offering professional development workshops through my local chapter that opened doors for me to conduct workshops at the national conferences. This ultimately led to me becoming the president of the San Francisco Bay Area chapter.

As the president, I made connections with recruiters, C-level executives of Fortune 500 companies, entrepreneurs and community and government leaders. It benefited my business while I was working in corporate and gave me exposure to so many powerful people that I felt I was truly six-degrees from anyone in the world. However, what I also discovered is the importance of maintaining those ties or they can become weak ones.

Working your network so that your connections remain strong takes time and a concerted effort. It's one thing to get the initial contact but it's another to build a long-term relationship. When effective networking takes place it's not a transactional relationship but a long-term synergistic strategic partnership. This takes time and commitment.

I'm not suggesting you have to call each other everyday but when it's mutually beneficial and genuine it will not be work but a pleasure to stay in touch. Technology and social media makes the effort more manageable. The challenge is when we have what's considered to be more of a one sided transaction. Meaning I asked you for a reference for a job and you provided it and that's the last time you heard from me. Versus, we have a natural relationship when we connected at a national conference. I recalled you worked at an organization where I'm looking to obtain a contract so I ask for a referral. You provide it and I send you a thank you card and continue keeping you informed of my progress and inquiring about how I may support your effort and this continues long term.

Associations can add powerful connections to your personal and business associations. The more you get involved, the more networking opportunities. The key is leveraging it based on your values and interests so you and your new contacts will already have a common starting point. Relentless follow-up with those connections will allow for both of you to fully benefit from the association.

YOUR PERSONALITY PROFILE

Understanding your natural profile can help you understand yourself so you can know how to connect better with others. Understanding how the world sees you and how you are wired can be leveraged for effective networking. Many people go to events to hand out business cards and call it networking because that is what they think they see others doing. They are duplicating someone else without taking time to better understand themselves and how they are perceived.

Some people are gregarious extroverts and others are introverts. Understanding yourself first can help you understand how to adjust your style as necessary depending on the personality you are attempting to network with at a function. It also gives you an indication of others' profiles so you can know how best to communicate in such a way that causes the desired response in them.

There are a variety of personality assessments such as Myers-Briggs Type Indicator®, DiSC, Strength Finder and Fascination Advantage® assessment. There are many other assessments as well. I'll highlight these four as I've taken all of them and have implemented them as a coach with clients and as a people leader in Corporate.

The Meyers Briggs Type Indicator® (MBTI)

This is considered to be the most widely used personality assessment in the world. It measures four pairs of opposing preferences that are inborn and value neutral to form a person's four-letter type. Type describes differences in how people approach the world, take in information and make decisions. Development and applications of psychological type are founded on the idea that understanding your type can help you appreciate your own strengths, gifts, and potential developmental needs, and help you understand and appreciate how other people may differ from you. Below is an outline of the categories and the potential options that each person may possess.

Your Preferred World or Attitude

E = Extraversion (Energized by interaction with others) or

I = Introversion (Energized by solitary activities)

Mental Process: Perception–Accessing/Gathering Info

S = Sensing (concrete, experiential awareness) or

N = Intuiting (abstract, symbolic awareness)

Mental Process: Judgment–Organizing/Evaluating/Deciding

T = Thinking (situations assessed objectively based on criteria) or

F = Feeling (situations assessed subjectively based on worth/values)

Orientation to the Outer World

J = Judging (plan ahead and follow the plan) or

P = Perceiving (keep options open to adapt)

Based on the assessment, my results identified me as an ENFJ. I am an extrovert, with a mental process of intuition, with a decision process of feeling and a judging orientation of how I see the world. Based on this information, I'm very comfortable at various networking functions and able to connect with all types of personalities. However, others who are more introverts might have to make more of a conscious effort to leverage their style to connect with others. This is helpful in assessing others who are different from me so I don't come across too strong that it turns them off.

DISC is a personality profile that uses a method for understanding behavior, temperament, and personality. It provides a comprehensive overview of the way that people think, act, and interact.

The DISC Personality Profile is based on the work of renowned psychologist Dr. William Moulton Marston, and was introduced in his 1928 book *"Emotions of Normal People."* William Marston, a contemporary of Carl Jung, developed the DISC Personality Profile after studying the personality traits, behavioral patterns, and instinctual reactions of thousands of individuals. As a result of his work, Marston developed the DISC assessment as a tool to measure four primary behavioral traits:

- **(D) Dominant:** Direct, outspoken, results-oriented, a leader, problem-solver
- **(I) Influencing:** Friendly, outgoing, talkative, optimistic, the life of the party, people-oriented

- **(S) Steady:** Team player, stable, consistent, maintains the status quo, peacemaker, family-oriented, patient
- **(C) Conscientious:** Logical, organized, data-driven, methodical, perfectionist, detail-oriented

The DiSC Personality Profile identifies patterns of behavior, and can be used to implement solutions for maximizing an individual's strengths and minimizing weaknesses. According to my DiSC results, my primary personality type is (I) Influencing and my overall results are I/DC. This indicates that I have a blend of inspiring, dominant and cautious traits. Some words that describe me from my DISC assessment are interactive, quick witted, results oriented and fast paced. This provides me with insights on how best to leverage my profile when networking with others.

The Clifton StrengthsFinder™ measures the presence of 34 talent themes. Talents are people's naturally recurring patterns of thought, feeling, or behavior that can be productively applied. The more dominant a theme is in a person, the greater the theme's impact on that person's behavior and performance. There are two books that highlight this concept. The first is by Marcus Buckingham and Donald Clifton with the Gallup Organization that is called *Now Discover Your Strengths* and an updated version called *StrengthsFinder 2.0* by Tom Rath of the Gallup Organization.

These books and the assessment with a focus on strengths based leadership are very helpful. The idea is to discover and learn to lead with your strengths versus spending time trying to be a "Jack of all trades and master of none." I recommend both books and taking the assessment to determine your strengths and how best to leverage them in building professional relationships. My top 5 results are Maximizer, Strategic, Relator, Significance and Activator.

Fascination Advantage® assessment is based on a book that I read by Sally Hogshead titled *How the World Sees You: Discover Your Highest Value Through the Science of Fascination*. The Fascination Advantage® Assessment will show how the world sees you at your best. It allows you to discover your natural communication advantages. On her website of how to fascinate, Sally Hogsheads states that this assessment is different from Meyers Briggs and StrengthsFinder in that this focuses on how the world sees you rather than how you see the world. The Fascination Advantage® measures the highest and best use of your personality brand.

The assessment provides you with your primary and secondary advantages. Combined, they call them your archetype. My primary advantage is prestige and my secondary is innovation. Therefore, my archetype is Avant-Guard. Three adjectives that describe how the world sees me are original, enterprising and forward thinking. When you communicate with your Primary and Secondary Advantages, you come across as more confident and authentic. This can provide you with great insight to leverage when connecting with others to build a relationship through networking.

ACCOUNTABILITY PARTNERS–EVERYONE ONE NEEDS A COACH, MENTOR AND SPONSOR

I define accountability in this context as the willingness to be transparent by sharing your personal and professional goals, tasks and assignments with specific people who will hold you to your commitments. When I say hold you to your commitments I'm referring to people who will call you out and will remind you of the consequences of not coming through on each of your obligations.

Many choose not to share what they are working on because they do not want to be held accountable to anyone. So if they change their mind or decide later they will not do something simply because no one else knows. Another consideration of accountability is having someone else look out for your best interests and help to guide you along the path of your desired endeavors. It helps to have a trusted go to person to bounce ideas off of and to obtain another perspective.

Having accountability partners makes a big difference in helping to achieve your objectives. I'll highlight three different types of accountability partners who can help make a positive difference in your career and life.

"A lot of people have gone further than they thought they could because someone else thought they could." –ZIG ZIGLAR

Coach

A coach is a great person to work with who can help you fulfill your goals. I'm partial to this type of accountability relationship since I'm an executive coach myself. There are different types of coaches and coaching relationships. Some are life coaches, others are executive coaches (which is what I consider myself) and others are internal company coaches. Coaching is a catalyzing relationship that accelerates the process of great performance. Coaches help their clients identify their purpose, they help bring out possibilities and help offer a journey of personal and professional discovery. Coaches are future oriented and can help you gain clarity for your pursuits. Individuals have hired me to help them through the process of fulfilling a long-term goal, identifying their strengths, determining career options, working through a challenging situation and getting promoted. Companies bring me in to do the same as well as group coaching and leadership workshops.

> "The greatest good you can do for another is not just to share your riches but to reveal to him his own." –Benjamin Disraeli

Mentor

A mentor is an influential leader who may be a subject matter expert. They are focused on helping you get up to speed in a certain area and may be assigned within an organization. Many people identify others who are doing what they aspire to do and ask for a mentoring relationship. Mentors can be considered as a wise counselor or an experienced leader who is willing to support others for a period of time. This is a common type of accountability partner relationship in corporate. Some of the core competencies of mentoring are they are known to challenge, support, empower and provide career direction.

> "Advice is like snow; the softer it falls, the longer it dwells upon, and the deeper it sinks into the mind."
> —Samuel Taylor Coleridge

Sponsor

A sponsor can be a senior level, influential supporter of an individual in a corporate environment. They tend to be a senior level representative of a high potential employee. A corporate sponsorship is a popular term that refers to a company paying for advertising at a public venue so they are associated with the event. It's a similar idea to be associated with a person of influence at a senior level. It's being connected to people or a person who is vetting for you as needed in meetings where you cannot attend. They represent you and your interests. This can be very helpful for your career when you have an internal senior level sponsor.

WHO'S THE DRIVER?

The key to all of these types of accountability partners is that you're the driver of the relationship. They are doing you the honor so ensure that you make it easy for them to continue this partnership. It's important that you take the responsibility to schedule the meetings or calls, you do the follow-up and you keep them abreast of the latest and greatest. The sooner you get it the better the engagement will be and the more value you will get. I have worked with many who have had mentors, sponsors or internal coaches where the relationship started out strong and over a period of time began to wane. When I would inquire about it, the response would be something related to the coach, mentor or sponsor not following up with them. If you take the responsibility for keeping the communication lines open and being flexible, you are less likely to be disappointed.

All of these are opportunities to build lasting and impactful relationships that can take your networking to another level. Applying this strategy allows you to be much more strategic and obtain your desired outcomes that are based on mutually beneficial relationships.

SUCCESS LEAVES CLUES

I borrowed this phrase from Anthony Robbins. The idea behind this is if you want to do anything or achieve a worthy goal, find someone who has already done it and learn from him or her because success leaves clues. As you are networking, do your homework on successful others. Leverage technology to conduct your research. You can find almost anything and anybody online and most are willing to share and if not, there are always books.

Many of my mentoring relationships are from people I've learned from without contacting them directly. Zig Ziglar,

Anthony Robbins, Brian Tracy, Stephen Covey and Jim Rohn, just to name a few. I've read their books where they all share recommendations on how they did what they did and explain that others can do the same. It's similar to a recipe for a meal. If you buy the same ingredients and follow the directions precisely, you should get the same results.

I'm known to cook really good pancakes. Not only does my family say so but I've also cooked for the men and boys at my church who say the same. The secret to my pancakes coming out perfectly is that I follow the directions exactly. Most tend to over stir the batter but if you pay attention to the directions, it specifically states not to over stir and to leave large lumps. I do this and it works.

You can use the same approach and find others who are doing what you aspire to do and apply the same principles. Now, I will admit that there may be other extenuating circumstances, external factors, environmental factors that could provide a different output. Just like using a frying pan instead of a griddle will give different results for pancakes even if the batter's exactly the same. Follow the principles and tweak for yourself as necessary and it should get you going in the right direction.

———~~~———

CHAPTER 10

Goal Setting Works!

"Setting goals is the first step in turning the invisible into the visible." —Tony Robbins

O VER THE YEARS, I've learned the significance of setting goals. I define a goal as a worthy endeavor in writing with a date. I've heard others define it as a dream with a deadline. All Fortune 500 companies establish goals based on their vision. I'm a believer in leveraging what works for large corporations and applying the same principles to us personally for our careers and life in general.

"What you get by achieving your goals is not as important as what you become by achieving your goals." –Zig Ziglar

GOAL SETTING WORKS!

I began to learn about the process of setting goals and their ful-fillment from reading many inspirational books and listening to many great speakers. Starting with the Bible where it states in Habakkuk, "Write the vision and make it plain." In Proverbs, "Without a vision people perish." I've read books by authors such as Jim Rohn, Steven Covey, Les Brown, Harvey MacKay, Dr. Norman Vincent Peal, Anthony Robbins, Brian Tracy and many others. Based on reading all of these books and applying the principles, I've seen it work for me multiple times through-out my life and am convinced of its power.

I also learned that all of these resources point to the same conclusion-goal setting works! I will share a few examples of how setting goals has worked for me.

Based on feeding on all the inspirational books, I decided to write my bucket list. However, I created it based on what I felt was my purpose. I believe in living on purpose and I want to ensure that my list connects to my vision and goals. My pur-pose is to help others maximize their potential. I accomplish this through speaking, teaching, coaching, writing, leading and training. Personal development is one of my core values so I enjoy the process of doing things to help enhance my gifts and talents.

I took time to dream about my ideal future without any limits and began to freely write a list in my journal. (I will have you go through the same process at the end of this chapter). My list included traveling abroad, writing books, conducting keynotes and motivational talks before large (thousands of people) audiences domestically and abroad, purchasing homes, cars and a variety of other nice and fun things.

I began with a high level list of all the things I would like to do, have and be. Then I drilled down on the list based on time spans of less than one year, between 1–3 years and over 3 years. I narrowed down my less than one-year list. As I listed the goal, I explored the steps it would take to make it a reality and established a timeline for those items to get as granular as possible.

One of the goals I decided to focus on in the first year bucket was improving my public speaking. This was a drill down on the vision of becoming a more effective communicator to help me be better equipped to lead and influence others. I always enjoyed speaking before groups of people and felt that it would help me be more effective in my sales role and better position me for leadership opportunities. Plus, my ultimate dream was to be a motivational speaker so focusing on being a speaker was a step toward fulfilling what I'm doing today.

I wrote out a strategy that included checking out local Toastmasters clubs, joining, getting involved and practicing my speaking. Toastmasters International has a communication and leadership curriculum and a process in place with various levels of achievement recognitions. I chose to focus on first obtaining my competent communication Toastmaster award. It required completing 10 speech projects focusing on various topics and ways of communicating. Each speech delivered is timed and evaluated based on Toastmasters criteria.

I joined a local club, immediately started signing up to speak and evaluate others. This made a big difference in my ability to learn to speak more effectively. I learned that I really enjoyed giving speeches so after completing my 10 presentations; I set a new goal to take the advanced program. From there I decided to compete in speech contests. This process stretched me and allowed me to learn from other great speakers. I won several speech contests over a period of a few years at the club, district, and regional level. It confirmed that I had a gift and I was happy to have set a goal to polish my gift.

THE GOAL SETTING PROCESS

Going through this goal setting process has led to me continuing to set new goals in various areas of my life. This one goal has been a door opener for me in getting promoted at American Express and Wells Fargo, going to work for a training company, becoming a facilitator for other companies and running my business of coaching, training and conducting leadership workshops. The power of a goal can make a major impact on your life. I'll walk you through the process.

JOURNALING

Journaling has been one of the most powerful tools that I've used for the past 20 years. It's provided me with a place to capture my thoughts, feelings, dreams, observations and aspirations. I recognize that many may think of it as a teenager's diary (that's good too) but it's so much more. It's your own book, customized with insights all about you. It's a great resource for meditation and reflection time. It allows you to think on paper. It's even more powerful when you read your past entries.

Imagine having the ability to pick up a book to read the details about the birth of your child, getting your first promotion, moving, getting married, going through a hard time, starting with a new company, a major trip or vacation, your thoughts from reading an inspirational book, thoughts after prayer, etc. Consider the impact of having your children reading your thoughts, ideas, plans, feelings, etc. It can be a source of inspiration for them and a key learning opportunity. Can you imagine having the opportunity to read your parents' journal entries from the past when they were your age or experienced similar challenges? It's like having a 30,000-foot perspective of your life and it helps you to better understand life's ups, downs and the balancing act to remain positive and encouraged to fulfill your purpose.

Writing in a journal can provide you with all of this and more. Since I've been writing in my journal I have all of these examples captured and whenever I need encouragement, I pick up any one of my journals and begin to read. I love capturing my thoughts, ideas, dreams and goals. It's amazing for me to read about what my dreams were 20 years ago and to see how many of those have been accomplished. It also let's me know if I'm on the right road based on what's in me because I have it all in writing.

Journal Exercise

- Purchase the best journal you can. A leather bound that you would enjoy using. It can be lined or unlined depending on your preference
- Begin with a header that includes the date, including the day of the week, the time and your location at the moment
    - As an example, I'll capture the current time, date, location, etc.
- Saturday, March 21, 2015 11:30am. Sitting outside at my daughter Jenay's swim meet at De La Salle High School in Concord, CA.

You can begin with anything you desire. Below are a few examples of how I like to begin many of my journal entries:

- I thank God that I had the opportunity this week of speaking at the National Sales Network. I spoke on the topic of The Audacity of HOPE. I received a lot of positive feedback and feel that this was one of my better talks. I felt on fire as I went through the acronym of HOPE …
- I just finished praying and would like to capture my thoughts and what's on my heart …
- I just returned from an off-site leadership team meeting with my VP and the other directors. It was a great meeting and I want to put in writing some of my take-a-ways …
- This week I hosted a team meeting in San Francisco. My agenda included a strength finder exercise, as I like to incorporate personal development into our team meetings …

270

- I returned from visiting my family in NJ and am grateful for the opportunity
- I just re-read my journal entries and realized I had not written in my journal during a hard time in my life. This is insightful to me because I noticed most all of my entries are related to good things or my future plans. However, when I was going through I wish I had captured my feelings during those times. This lets me know the importance of writing during the good and the bad as I learn from them all…

Now, it's your turn. I recommend that you start by writing your current state of being. Meaning your current situation. Where are you living, what are you doing professionally with your career, family life, things going on in your life today, etc? Then write your desired state. Meaning what's next for you. What else do you want in life? Consider various areas, including some of the following:

- Physical and Emotional Health
- Family
- Spiritual
- Career

Take your time and stretch yourself by capturing those areas if time and money were not an issue. Think about it first then put ink to paper with all of your ideas and thoughts.

PURPOSE LEADS TO VISION

Purpose is the reason for a thing; why something was created. I think it can be illuminating to conduct various exercises to gain insight into our purpose and mission. Personally, I believe in prayer and reading the Bible. I consider God my ultimate manufacturer and the Bible as an owner's manual. Additionally, you can gain insights by reviewing your life based on what you love doing, being and having.

The following is an exercise that I like to refer to as "Back to the Future." Similar to the movie, it allows us to revisit our past for key learnings. Then leverage those insights to make decisions around a forecast of our future. Reflect on what you enjoyed most from the various times in your past life. Begin with where you are today. What is it that you love in this current season of your life? This should be only about what's happening in your life today. Not what you are hoping for or anticipate happening. The question is what is it in your life that you currently love on today's date. Think about your situation in terms of who are you with, where are you working, where are you living, what are your extracurricular activities, children, health, etc.

You may write at the top of a page in your journal and center the following phrase: "What I Love." Then three column headings under it that are "Being, Doing, Having." Your responses should be captured in one word or short phrases in bullet form.

Now, that you've captured what you love currently, continue with the exercise by writing what you loved being, doing and having during the following periods in your life:

- Childhood
- Teenage years
- College years or 18–23
- Your mid-late 20s
- 30s
- 40s+ or/and up to your current age

It's important that you pause through the various age periods and reflect. Look for similar things and ideas that pop-up repetitively. What trends are you noticing? Capture your insights and thoughts as you reflect on your list.

Is there anything that you loved doing in the past that if you had the time and resources that would make a positive difference in your life today if you restarted it? If so, write those things in your journal and explore what it would take to incorporate it. Maybe, you may have to exchange it for a habit that's not supporting your dreams and goals.

One of my observations when I first went through this exercise was that I loved riding my bike as a child and teenager but I had not done so in years. I have kids and thought it would be a great idea for us to ride together so I added it back into my schedule and it replaced watching television with the kids.

VISION TO GOALS

The next step with this exercise is based on your past reflections and assessing your current situation. If you desire different results in your life, you will need to make the appropriate adjustments. If you're on track to what you ultimately desire then continue on the same track.

Hopefully, based on reading all the other chapters, you see the importance of doing things differently to get the results you desire.

Think about what you want out of your life and what it will take to get there from your current assessment. Now, forecast if all goes according to plan, what is it in your life that you will love being, doing and having in the next 10 years and write it down. Continue to forecast in 10–20 year increments until we get to the age we would like to live.

The last step in the process is to go to the age you'd like to be when you die. Write your obituary from the perspective of what you would like people to say about you. (Similar to *Time is Ticking!* in Chapter 2). What do you want to be said about you by your family (spouse, kids, siblings, etc.), your friends, coworkers, someone in the community. Envision who would say what but gear it towards what you would like to be stated. The objective is to think about it in advance in order to live it out so it becomes a reality. This also will provide you with insights about yourself and what really matters most to you.

GOALS TO ACTION STEPS

As a result of this exercise, what is it that you would like to have, be and do? Review your list and circle all that resonate most with you. The next step is to prioritize all the words and phrases circled to categorize them. Which of those circled on the list would you like to do in the next 12 months? Which would you target to complete in 1–3 years? Finally, which would you place in the bucket beyond 3 years?

Let's begin with a focus on those items you would like to complete in the next 12 months. Narrow this short-term list into a prioritized list of your top 5–10 goals. Take the top 5 goals and get more granular by converting them to SMART goals. This stands for Specific, Measurable, Attainable, Realistic and Time bound.

George T. Doran is given credit for first presenting SMART goals in the November 1981 issue of Management Review. The paper was titled "There's a SMART way to write management's goals and objectives," according to Ask.com.

As an example, let's say one of my goals that I would like to achieve in the next 12 months is to write a book. Now, I'll convert that to a SMART goal:

- **Specific:** I will write a coaching book focused on career development strategies for individual contributors and middle level managers

- **Measurable:** I will write 1 chapter per month of at least 10 pages in Word per chapter for a total of 10 chapters plus an introduction and coaching exercises

- **Achievable:** This is doable based on my current schedule

- **Realistic:** Writing a 10 chapter book is realistic for me because the chapters are based primarily on speeches I give to large audiences

- **Time Bound:** I've completed 5 chapters and am half way through the 6th chapter. I will complete all 10 chapters by August 30, 2016, and today is March 23, 2016. I'm committed to writing every day for at least 30 minutes.

SMART is a part of the preparation process. In order to achieve a worthy goal we have to prepare to get there or it will not happen. Now, it's your turn to convert your top 5 lists of goals into SMART goals.

ACTION STEPS TO RESULTS

Take your top 5 SMART goals and work your plan. Decide of the 5 SMART goals, which one will make the biggest impact and provide you with the most traction. That's where you focus most of your time and effort and it's the goal you start with to completion.

As an example, of my top 5 goals that include writing a book, updating my website, obtaining more speaking engagements with national organizations, getting more training business and growing my coaching business. I believe writing my book would have the biggest impact and can positively help me and lead to the achievement of my other goals. Therefore, my focus goes towards the completion of the book first.

Determine your first priority goal and commit to completing it by your established deadline. Be sure to take time to celebrate when you complete your first goal in order to maintain the momentum and to build on your success.

MOTIVATION AND AIDS TO STAY THE COURSE

When you are endeavoring to fulfill a dream you will have distractions and challenges. Understand it's part of the process. You have the ability to move things in your favor to help you remain focused.

I recommend that you feed on positive things that will help you remain motivated. When I state the word feed, I mean what we are putting into our brain and heart through our senses. As the saying goes, "You are what you eat." It's true in the natural as well as mental. Consider the books we read, television shows we watch, type of music we listen to and other media we allow to get our attention.

It's similar to how television advertising works to subliminally change our thought process to desire their product or service. Depending on how often we are exposed will determine our level of desire for it. This is why as of today, I can still tell you that a Big Mac is two all beef patties, special sauce, lettuce, cheese, pickles, onions on a sesame seed bun. It's because as a kid, I heard a commercial with those lyrics over and over and over.

Here's a test, see if you can complete the following sentences or guess the product:

- "Like a good neighbor _____ _____ is there"
- "Snap, crackle, _____"
- "Priceless"
- "I'm loving it"
- "I'd like to teach the world to sing"

- "_____ _ _____ the San Francisco treat!"
- "The best part of waking up is _____ in your cup"
- "I want my baby back, baby back, baby back …
  _____ baby back ribs"
- "I don't wanna grow up, 'cause maybe if I did,
  I couldn't be a ____ _ ____ kid."
- Gimme a break, gimme a break, break me off a piece of
  that ____ ____ bar"

So, how did you do? I'm guessing that you got most right if not all of them. Why is that? I'm sure you have some great points. Let me add a few thoughts. I believe it's a combination of the repetition of hearing and seeing it over and over. Plus, the jingle adds an element to impact our emotions and to make it easy to recall. Then they connect it to a product to cause us to want it. All of these ads were considered very effective. These are powerful tools to cause people to purchase a product. I suggest we leverage what works in advertising and apply it to maintaining momentum as we are in the pursuit of our goals.

Create a vision board. A vision board is a tool that can be used to help you clarify, concentrate and maintain focus on the attainment of your specific goals. It's any type of board you choose to use that allows you to display images of what you desire to be, do and have in life. The idea behind a vision board is to have examples or representations of your goal in front of you so you are seeing it all the time. This literally keeps your goal in front of you that helps it to remain a focus.

"Imagination is everything. It's a preview of life's coming attractions" —ALBERT EINSTEIN

Take time daily to envision your goal fulfilled. See yourself living out your goal and go through the entire experience in your mind's eye. Hold on to this feeling and use your imagination to recall it at will. It's similar to the process we go through when we worry. It's a form of meditation. We can use it for the positive or negative. When we are concerned, we are constantly thinking things over in our minds. In many cases we see it through as a worst-case scenario over and over. This is what leads to worry; constantly feeding on the negative.

I recommend we use the same process for what we want. Using it for the positive to focus on our goals. Just as we use our imagination that leads to worry, we can use our imagination to lead to the fulfillment of our goals.

I'd like you to go through the following exercise. Close your eyes and imagine it's one year from today and you are living out the fulfillment of your top 1-year goals. You went through the process I outlined and it worked! Imagine you're living in it. What are you wearing? Who are you with? How does it make you feel to have fulfilled your goals? Hold on to that feeling for a moment and enjoy knowing that it's accomplished. You got the job, the position, the raise, the business, etc.

You may now open your eyes, but keep the thought, feelings and emotions. Now, capture your experience with this exercise in your journal. Write how it made you feel. Describe in as much detail as possible the what, who, where, when and why of your goals being fulfilled.

There is a Part 2 of this exercise. Now, I'd like you to close your eyes and imagine it's one year from now. This time, see yourself in the future having been exposed to this process of goal setting but not completing the exercise and as a result not having accomplished your goal. You know how it is, you had good intentions but life happened. Things came up and you were not able to fulfill your short-term goals. Knowing that you've been down this path before and have read similar types of books and you're still on the "someday" isle. Remember, with your eyes still closed, that you are living this out on the canvas of your imagination. Whatever today's date is for you, it's one year from now. You have not completed any of your 1-year goals. How does this make you feel? Please capture your emotions and feelings for it being a year later and you have not completed your goals.

Finally, think about both scenarios of completing your goals in one year and not having completed them. If you are fully persuaded to go for your goals no matter what, then I've done my job. If you're not quite there, then please take a break and revisit this exercise at a later time. If you're still not there then give this book to a friend. Recognize that you will have many challenges and obstacles as you go for the attainment of your goals. It is part of the process and it's critical that you remain committed to the process of fulfilling your goals. Having a strong desire can help but having an unwavering commitment is even more important to you fulfilling your dreams.

Has there been anything in your life that you wanted really bad and you persevered through obstacles and challenges to get it? There are a few examples that come to mind for me. When I moved to California in 2004 and was looking for a job in corporate, my goal was to get a similar role that I had with American Express of leading a sales team. I posted for a vice president of business banking position that was a leadership role. I started my sales career outside of college working in manufacturing sales. After I obtained my MBA I began working in financial services for American Express in sales. When I transitioned from manufacturing sales to service sales, it was a breath of fresh air for me. I could relate much better to the industry, the employees and the customer base.

So, when I came to California, I felt my ideal position was a sales leadership position in the financial service industry. I targeted Wells Fargo in San Francisco. I leveraged my network of contacts that worked for Wells to help me once I found a position posted that fit my criteria. I found the VP of business banking position on their website and posted. I received a call within one week of posting from the HR recruiter who screened me. I felt very confident during my interview based on my previous experiences working with Amex as well as my presentation skills. I leveraged my strengths to obtain a recommendation from the recruiter to the next level and had a phone interview with the decision maker. I did my homework prior to meeting with the decision maker. I asked others who work for Wells to let me know any information. LinkedIn was not widely used in 2004 since it was founded in 2002, so I had to go the old fashioned way of asking others and doing research online. I learned the decision maker was an executive vice president and I felt very comfortable working and presenting to senior level leaders. I had previous experience training C level executives on presentation skills. In addition, I had previous working exposure for other EVPs and presidents.

Based on my experience and strengths, I was able to make a personal connection during the interview and felt confident I'd get the job. However, I was later informed the EVP wanted me to interview with a market president in the retail group of Wells Fargo. This role I applied for was in the business banking group but they work directly with the retail team.

I went through the same process to prepare for the interview with the market president and that went well. Then I got the call with the news that they decided to offer the position I posted for to an internal candidate. However, they wanted to offer me a position of strategy manager, reporting directly to the EVP. It wasn't the position I posted for but it was a foot in the door. I positioned my response before accepting the offer to ask what would I need to do to get the position in which I posted. They let me know this was a lead in role for the position so I accepted.

My goal was still to become the VP so I leveraged my role as strategy manager by coming in earlier than the EVP and staying later than her at the office. This allowed me to have great after hour conversations with my EVP. It helped to strengthen our relationship and her trust in me as a leader. I went overboard to come up with innovative ideas for the role and I ensured that I made her look good as the EVP. I reached out to all those who had the spot I wanted and I scheduled lunch meetings with them to pick their brain on what it takes to be successful in that role. I also shadowed them during meetings and review sessions. I always shared my key learnings with the EVP.

After 7 months with Wells Fargo, I was promoted to vice president of business banking in the San Francisco Bay area. This was a goal I set and mapped out a strategy and worked it until I obtained my desired position. Regardless of the challenges and obstacles, I kept the goal as my goal. After being offered a different position originally, I could have got discouraged and not accepted the strategy manager position. Or I could have taken that role but not pursued my ultimate goal. It demonstrated to me that persistence pays off. Remaining focused and committed to your goals can and will be worth the effort.

Desire is another factor in the attainment of goals. Having a strong "want to" makes a big difference in what's accomplished. You will be filled to the level of your thirst for a SMART goal. How bad do you want it? How pressed are you to achieve the goal? The more intense your hunger, the stronger your desire to satisfy it.

What are some examples of goals you've had in the past and really wanted and almost seemed impossible but came to pass? Take time to think about it and capture your examples in your journal.

An example that I'll share was a goal for me to attend Howard

University to obtain my bachelors degree. After high school I attended my local community college with the goal of transferring to Howard University after two years. I wanted to major in marketing at Howard University so part of my preparation was to take the classes at the community college that would best prepare me for Howard. I also recall speaking with an advisor at my community college to get their input on what I should do to improve my chances of getting into Howard. I understood having strong grades would help but I felt that was only the status quo. This is what all transfer students are doing but I wanted to determine what I could do to better distinguish myself. I was informed that getting involved in my local community college could help. As a result I volunteered and was selected to become a peer counselor. This gave me leadership experience to help other college students at the community college. In addition, I had to work as a student and had obtained experience working at McDonald's and at AT&T.

A year and a half later, I applied to Howard University and was accepted! However, that's when the hard part began. I did not have enough money to attend. I recall praying to God for help because I really wanted to go and was willing to do whatever it took to be able to attend now that I was accepted. I also had been saving money from my job but it was not enough. I applied for student loans and still did not have enough. I had purchased a new car about 6 months prior to being accepted and was making monthly payments. I thought this money could be going towards my education rather than a depreciating asset of a new car. I had such a strong desire to attend Howard that I made a conscious decision to give back my car to the finance company as a voluntary repossession. I was desperate and really determined to attend Howard University. I believed that I would not only attend, but graduate from Howard University and that it set me up to do great things.

Time was running out and it was time for new students to go for the orientation process, completing final registration, getting housing, etc. Before having all the money, I went to Howard University believing it would work out. I gave them all the money I had plus the student loans and was still a bit short.

Shortly after I started classes and the final deadline for payment was due, my mother obtained some unexpected money to help me pay and it got me over the hump to attend, thank God!

Are you willing to go to that extent to achieve your top goal? If so, you're on your way! If not, find something you can get that hungry over pursuing and give it all you have. Go for it!

Conclusion

"Whether you think you can, or you think you can't—you're right." —Henry Ford

Congratulations for getting to the end of this book. My desire is that this book became a wake-up call for you to take full responsibility for your career, that you see your current work situation in a new light and that it inspired you to strategically develop a plan of action that leverages the best of you. This book provided a culmination of examples from my experiences working in management roles in corporate to coaching all levels of professionals to leadership development strategies and ideas. Now, it's your turn to take action on what you learned. Review your notes and decide what's one thing you will do now as an act of faith that will allow you to maximize what you've read. I don't want this to be just another book that you read and it goes on the bookshelf. I would like this to be a reference book that you go back to like a tool in your toolbox.

In order to breathe life into a situation, it takes repetition and a saturation of inspiring information to help renew your approach and perspective to your work.

THE "YEAH, BUTS ..."

When I went through my coaching training with Coach U, I learned that most people have their moments of "yeah, but ..." Have you every attended a seminar and learn new ideas that excite you and you are looking forward to applying the new insights learned, but after you get home you begin to think through your new implementation plan and thoughts of how to and where do I begin come to mind? How am I going to do this? How will this work out with my already hectic schedule? How will trying this new approach really change anything? I call these types of questions the, "yeah, buts." It's essentially saying, I like what I read and learned and yeah, it's good stuff conceptually but how will I be able to sustain it in my work environment? It's all the reasons why it will be challenging to leverage the recommendations in this book.

Beware of the yeah, buts and know that they are part of the process of pursuing a worthy endeavor. I will venture to write that most of the concepts you read in this book are familiar and you probably heard or read of many of them before. Sometimes it takes us hearing and reading certain concepts over and over before we actually take action. The point is to take action and you can choose to do so now so you don't have to repeat the same mistakes or stay in the same place any longer. The choice is yours. I recommend not allowing the past cycle to continue to repeat itself but that you choose to take action on this information now, rather than later. A lesson not learned will be repeated so learn all you can now.

Stephen Covey said, "To know and not to do is not to know." This is for those of you who may say you already know this stuff and you're fine with your current situation. If you are not applying what you read and learned then you really have not learned it. I'm asking you to acknowledge your concerns and limiting beliefs of your, "yeah buts." A great approach to overcoming them is raising them to the surface by writing them out. This allows you the opportunity to identify and address them directly.

You may fill out the chart on the next page and use that as a way of brainstorming with others to help identify solutions to overcome your *yeah, buts.*

Action Idea*	Yeah Buts/ Limiting Beliefs	Solutions
Join Toastmasters to improve my presentation skills	Time to do it. I have a full time job and 3 young kids with activities.	• Identify clubs near me that meet during the lunch hour • Brainstorm with my spouse on other options

* Example for illustrative purposes

NEVER STOP LEARNING

When I was in undergraduate, I remember being excited to get to my junior year of college so I could take all classes in my major. I felt like most of high school and my first few years of undergraduate there were required courses that I was not as interested in learning about. I majored in marketing and was very interested in taking and learning about marketing management, marketing research, advertising and sales and other marketing related classes. I tended to do better in areas of interest because I was genuinely interested in most of the major classes. I felt the same way when I obtained my MBA and performed even better since I had a few more years of work experience that helped make the classes more relevant for me.

Since completing my MBA, I wanted to stay fresh in my professional development pursuits so I would read mostly business books. I had an appetite for learning and it's stayed with me over the years. It's made a tremendous difference for me gaining knowledge and I'm surprised how much information I've retained and been able to apply in my various professional roles. I believe all the reading I've done over the years allowed me to become a more effective leader in the corporate environment and helped when starting my own business.

I would like to encourage you to make reading a regular part of your professional development strategy. There are books written on just about any topic you can think of today. Whatever your goal, you can find a book about someone who has done what you aspire to do and you can learn from them and use their information to motivate you. Ensure you learn from others but stay true to yourself so you remain authentic.

Personal development is critical to remain competitive. I want to highlight this so you recognize the importance of continuing your education. It's important to understand anything you do to improve yourself will provide you with a competitive advantage. The primary purpose should be to become the best you but it also has benefits for job interviews, promotions and provides you with additional things to differentiate you from the crowd. Leaders are readers and readers are leaders. Choose to become and remain a leader who continually remains fresh and relevant.

Leverage technology to make it easier for you to make the

most of your time. Kindle, books on CD, podcasts, YouTube and blogs can all make a difference in your quest to gain usable information. I use my drive time to listen to books on CD, I use my airplane time to read books and my downtime to read or listen to TED Talks of interest. You can always leverage idle time as learning time.

There are some interesting statistics that I want to share regarding reading. Review the chart below and think about how your results compare. As a way to differentiate yourself in a positive manner, consider a reading strategy that will help you stand out from the majority.

According to Static Brain Research Institute:

- 33% — Total percent of U.S. high school graduates who will never read a book after high school
- 42% — Total percentage of college students who will never read another book after they graduate
- 80% — Total percentage of U.S. families who did not buy a book this year
- 70% — Total percentage of adults that have not been in a book store in the past 5 years
- 57% — Total percentage of books started that aren't read to completion

FOUR STAGES OF LEARNING

As you begin to take action on making changes to implement key learning points from reading this book I want to introduce you to the four stages of learning. It's also referred to as The

Conscious Competence Learning Model. I was introduced to this model while attending UCLA Anderson School of Management, Management Development for Entrepreneurs program. It was like attending an accelerated MBA program for small business owners. The purpose of me sharing this with you is to help manage your expectations as you implement the strategies you obtained from reading this book. There is a process that we all go through and the better we understand this as a normal part of learning, we will be able to continue in the process as we run into challenges.

The four stages of learning any new skill is credited to being developed by Noel Burch who was an employee of the GTI Corporation. The four stages of learning are: unconsciously incompetent, consciously incompetent, consciously competent and unconsciously competent.

1. Unconsciously Incompetent — This is the stage in the learning process when you don't know what you don't know. As an example, you decide to implement improving your executive presence and you determine from your self-assessment that you want to improve in the area of becoming more analytical. You begin analyzing some reports and you discuss your analysis on your next one on one with your leader who clarifies some of your analysis to help you look at the data in a new light. You think you have it down but you soon discover that you may want to work with another who's considered a propeller head.

2. Consciously Incompetent — In this stage you become aware of your deficiencies. You now realize that you don't know it all in this new area of interest that causes you to seek input from other subject matter experts.

3. Consciously Competent — Continuing with the example of wanting to improve your executive image in the area of analytics, you have been working with the propeller head/aka the subject matter expert in your group and discussing your findings on your one on ones with you leader and are now comfortable doing the analysis. You now know which reports to pull and how best to manipulate the data for your needs. You are now competent in the area of analytics and you're aware of your enhancement. You are following the script each time you analyze reports and it's working for you.

4. Unconsciously Competent — This is the final stage where you are now flowing. You can do the analysis without giving much thought to it like driving home from your office. It's now second nature and you have it down so much so that you don't need a script to follow nor a propeller head to help.

Let this model be an encouragement for you to continue through the process of choosing areas to focus improving. As you go through the learning process for each new idea let it be the momentum to continue making this a regular process so you become unconsciously competent in all areas that you identified.

CLOSING THOUGHT

You are stepping into greatness. You are a unique, one of a kind individual the world has never seen before. You were born to do great things. You've always been special. When you came into the world, there was a mark of greatness stamped upon your life. You were born to succeed in every role you assume in your career and in your personal life. Decide to be the best you, leverage the information in this book and go for being, doing and having over the top results in all areas of your life!

Now capture your key thoughts and take-a-ways from reading this book:

_____

_____

_____

_____

_____

_____

_____

_____

_____

_____